THE EXCELLENCE

OF

REVEALED RELIGION

T0382328

CAMBRIDGE UNIVERSITY PRESS
Cambridge, New York, Melbourne, Madrid, Cape Town,
Singapore, São Paulo, Delhi, Mexico City

Cambridge University Press
The Edinburgh Building, Cambridge CB2 8RU, UK

Published in the United States of America by Cambridge University Press, New York

www.cambridge.org
Information on this title: www.cambridge.org/9781107662216

First published 1928
First paperback edition 2013

A catalogue record for this publication is available from the British Library

ISBN 978-1-107-66221-6 Paperback

THE EXCELLENCE
OF
REVEALED RELIGION

*An Enquiry into the Meaning
of Revelation*

BY

C. G. CHALLENGER, M.A.

*formerly Scholar of Peterhouse, and
Lady Kay Scholar of Jesus College*

THE
HULSEAN PRIZE ESSAY
1927

CAMBRIDGE
AT THE UNIVERSITY PRESS
1928

To

MY FATHER & MOTHER

PREFACE

IN 1790, the Reverend John Hulse, B.A., of St John's College, Cambridge, left a considerable benefaction to endow a grand scheme for the defence of the Christian Faith[1].

The benefaction was divided into four separate endowments[2]:

(i) The endowment of an annual prize for "the best Dissertation on the evidence in general, or on the prophecies and miracles in particular, or any other particular argument, whether the same be direct or

---

[1] The scheme is drawn up in Hulse's will, of which Parkinson (*Hulsean Lectures*, 1838, p. xxxi) says: "This extraordinary document, as it must evidently have occupied the thoughts of Mr Hulse for nearly the whole of his long life, so must the composition of it have formed the (probably most agreeable) employment of a considerable proportion of it."

Hulse's motive for his benefaction is thus represented by Christopher Benson, the first Hulsean Lecturer (1819): "He lived in an age when infidel notions were especially rife throughout the land, and when unbelief seemed to have before it a clearer prospect of final triumph than has either before or since attended its malignant efforts. He felt moreover how inefficiently he had (from causes which he could not control) discharged his own spiritual functions: and sought by these means to effect through the agency of others the good ends which he could so well design, though physical rather than spiritual and mental weakness had deprived him of the power to execute them." (Parkinson, *op. cit.* p. xxxiii.)

[2] *Ibid.* p. xxxiii ff.

collateral proofs of the Christian or revealed religion, in order to evince its truth and excellence[1]."

(ii) The endowment of the office of Christian Advocate, a "learned and ingenious person, who is to compose yearly some proper and judicious answer or answers to...new and popular or other cavils and objections against the Christian or Revealed religion, or against the Religion of Nature....Such his answers to be...against notorious infidels, whether atheists or deists...[2]."

(iii) The endowment of a Lectureship for the delivering of twenty lectures or sermons annually, "the subject of which discourses shall be as followeth: ...to shew the evidence for revealed religion, and to demonstrate in the most convincing and persuasive manner the truth and excellence of Christianity, so as to include not only the prophecies and miracles, general and particular, but also any other proper or useful arguments, whether the same be direct or collateral proofs of the Christian religion..."

(iv) The endowment of four divinity scholarships at St John's College[3].

[1] Benson thought that this prize "was intended by the Founder to stimulate the industry of the slumbering (sic) and to draw forth latent talent in defence of the Gospel." Parkinson, ibid.

[2] The Advocate was also to have the duty of helping members of the University in their private religious difficulties.

[3] *Subsequent history of the scheme.* There was great difficulty in filling the Lectureship on account of the excessive number of lectures (20) to be given. The first Lecturer was not appointed till 1819. In 1830 the number of lectures was reduced to *eight*, on a petition in Chancery. In 1860, by a statute confirmed by the Queen in Council, the number was

From the phraseology of Mr Hulse's will
can be reconstructed in outline his religious
Weltanschauung. There are for him, it seems,
two classes of religion, the *Religion of Nature* and
Revealed Religion. Christianity exhausts the latter
class. The *truth and excellence* of the Christian or
Revealed Religion is capable of being *demonstrated* by means of *proofs* or *evidence*. There are
two types of proof, *direct* and *collateral*, and
prophecies and miracles belong to one or other of
these groups. Finally, anti-Christian polemic is
regarded as consisting of *objections and cavils*.

The present Essay is an attempt to trace the
growth and decay of this religious outlook. As
this outlook is based upon a particular conception
of Revelation, the enquiry resolves itself into an
attempt to trace the growth of what we have
ventured to call the *classical*[1] view of Revelation;
to criticise this view; and to contrast with it the
modern conception of Revelation.

The Essay falls, accordingly, into two parts:
an examination of the growth and decay of
the classical view, with its peculiar type of
apologetic; and an attempt to discover the
modern conception of Revelation and the type
of apologetic proper to it.

further reduced to *four*. At the same time the office of
Christian Advocate was replaced by that of Hulsean Professor
of Divinity.

[1] On the analogy of Einstein's phrase "the classical theory
of Mechanics." The epithet seemed a more convenient one
than "hard-and-fast."

In the early history of the Christian religion
we find a double development. There is, in the
first place, the growth among Christians of a
definite attitude towards the historical documents
of their Faith, and, secondly, the growth of an
attitude towards current non-Christian thought.
The first of these lines of development leads to
the conception of Christianity as a Revealed
Religion, and the second to the conception of a
natural enlightenment. The history of the
relations of these two sources of knowledge may
be divided into three periods. We shall try to
shew how the first Christian theologians define
their position with regard to Philosophy, how
this Philosophy becomes the Reason of the
Middle Ages, and how Reason when it once
more becomes enfranchised is employed as the
basis for a Natural Religion which is set over
against Christianity.

"Whoever would take the religious literature
of the present day as a whole, and endeavour
to make out clearly on what basis Revelation is
supposed by it to rest...would probably find that
he had undertaken a perplexing but not altogether
profitless enquiry." So wrote Mark Pattison at
the end of his article in *Essays and Reviews*.
Adequately to do this for the present day would
be a laborious task, but we have tried to indicate
the results to which such an enquiry would
probably lead.

C. G. C.

CONTENTS

Preface . . . . . . page v

PART I

Chap. I. *The Catholic Conception of Revelation* I

Early Christian "sources of faith" : (1) The Old
Testament : theory of inspiration. (2) The teaching of
Christ and the Apostles. Development of a New Testament
scripture. Equal authority with the Old. Allegorism.
"The Bible." (3) Prophecy. Its decline. Revival in
Montanism. Supplanted by ecclesiastical authority.
Summary.   •

Chap. II. *Christianity and Philosophy* . 10

Philosophy in the Roman Empire. The educated
Christian. Relations between Christianity and Philosophy : (1) First period (subordination of Christianity
to Philosophy) : The Apologists. Their problems.
Justin. (2) Second period (equality of Christianity and
Philosophy) : Clement, Origen, Tertullian. (3) Third
period (subordination of Philosophy) : Philosophy
becomes "Reason." Augustine. Summary.

Chap. III. *Faith and Reason* . . . 20

The Dark Ages. Erigena. Scholasticism. Relation of
Reason to Faith : (1) First period : Reason the hand-
maid of Faith. Progress of Philosophy. "Credo ut
intellegam." (2) Second period : Rediscovery of
Aristotle. Aristotle and Christ : attempts at reconciliation. The two spheres : Albertus Magnus. "The
Scholastic Synthesis" : Thomas Aquinas. (3) Third
period : Decay of the Synthesis. Duns Scotus. William
of Occam. Summary.

Chap. IV. *Natural and Revealed Religion* page 31

The Reformation. Search for a new authority. "Reason." The Religion of Nature. Is Revelation necessary? Is Revelation true? Rationalist apologetic. Old Bailey Theology. Paley's *Evidences*. Their relation to Hulse's apologetic scheme.

Chap. V. *Critique of the Classical Theory of Revelation* . . . 44

Recapitulation. Decay of the classical theory: a new world-view. Examination of the Paleyan Apologetic: Miracles: modern attitude. Miracles as evidences. The value of testimony. Paley's presuppositions: "positive, external" Revelation; its supposed purpose. Revelation cannot be a body of facts. The plain man. Prolegomena to a modern theory.

PART II

Chap. VI. *The Mode of Revelation* . . 57

Adumbrations in history of a truer theory. No Revelation without human effort. The quest for knowledge of the Divine: (1) Practical knowledge: divination. (2) Theoretical: mythology, theology. Hebrew prophecy—a unique synthesis. "Prophecy" the mode of Revelation.

Chap. VII. *Creative Inspiration* . . 73

"Continuity" of Prophets' and Believers' experience. Creative Inspiration: what is it? I. Alleged direct inspiration: (1) "The breath of Yahweh." (2) Mystical experience. II. Religious knowledge as an interpretation. (1) Of subjective phenomena: the moral life, religious experience itself. Mysticism. (2) Of objective phenomena: History, Nature. Revelation given in all these spheres. "The faculty of divination." Schleiermacher, Otto.

Chap. VIII. *The Excellence of Revealed Religion* . . page 91

Religion can be styled "revealed" in respect of its character as the product of Prophecy. The modern form of apologetic for Revelation is the vindication of religious experience. "From God to God."

Bibliography 98

PART ONE

CHAPTER I

The Catholic Conception of Revelation

THE first Christians regarded themselves as the
new "Israel of God[1]." Christ had come as
the Messiah to save the Jews in general, but had
been rejected by them; only a small remnant had
received Him. But this remnant was still Jewish.
It carried over into the new faith Jewish modes
of thought and Jewish modes of worship. So it
continued to worship in the temple and to use
the Jewish scriptures. These were for it ἡ γραφή
—the writing *par excellence*[2]. But the New Israel
were "Christians" in virtue of possessing a further revelation of God in the teaching of Christ.
Besides this they had the oral teaching of the
apostles, and the utterances of the Christian prophets. There were therefore, we can say, three
"sources of faith" in the earliest church: (1) the
Old Testament Scripture, (2) the teaching of
Christ as expounded by the apostles, (3) the
Christian prophets.

The first of these sources is of a different
character from the other two. In the first place,

---

[1] Galatians, vi, 16.   [2] Cp. 1 Corinthians, xv, 3.

scripture was a written and definite authority. Some centuries of work had gone to determine the correct text. Secondly, it was regarded as verbally inspired—every word, every "jot and tittle" had been dictated by the Spirit of Yahweh. It formed the direct Revelation of God to man. There had naturally grown up a body of scholars whose work it was to elucidate the text, to make available the Revelation by applying it to the needs of life. It had been the work of the Rabbinic schools to formulate the necessary principles of exegesis. Thus Hillel had formulated seven rules[1] by which the traditions necessary to a priestly religion could be deduced from the Scriptures. Later Philo introduced a new system of interpretation, the allegorical method. It is important to notice the attitude of the Jews towards their scripture, for the history of the Christian use of scripture is determined by it. *The growth of the Christian oral traditions into a written canon is an assimilation of them to the status and character of the Jewish scriptures.* How this change took place we must now consider.

The teaching of Christ and of the apostles, at first transmitted orally, came soon to be written down. The apostles found it necessary to write to the churches they had planted, since they could not always be present with them. They also wrote down or dictated their "memoirs" (ὑπομνήματα). At the same time there grew up

[1] F. W. Farrar, *A History of Interpretation*, Lecture II.

a collection of the sayings (λόγια) of Jesus, corresponding to the collections of the sayings of the Jewish Rabbis such as are found in the *Pirqe Aboth*. A little later these two types of Christian literature, the memoirs and the sayings, were used as sources for "Gospels"—records giving a life of Jesus for the use of some particular Christian community.

So long as the apostles themselves and the "apostolic men" who were their disciples still survived, the written records were not *unique*—they were open to correction by living actors in the scenes they depicted. But as time went on, they necessarily acquired a special value as first-hand accounts written at the time of a particular outpouring of the Holy Spirit.

There were many accounts[1] and many alleged apostolic epistles in circulation, so that it soon became necessary to decide which of them were to be regarded as authoritative. A process of "pruning" began, guided by the principle that only those writings which were proved to be the work of apostles or apostolic men were to be selected[2]. This process went on for a long time, but by 200 A.D. the canon was more or less fixed.

There was now a New Testament as well as an Old Testament canon, and the attitude of Christians towards the New Testament became

[1] Cp. Luke, i, 1.
[2] B. J. Kidd, *A History of the Church to* 461 A.D., I, pp. 271 ff.

4

identical with their attitude towards the Old[1]. As early as the time of the Apostolic Fathers we find an equal authority attributed to the words of Christ and those of the apostles. Later one of the Apologists, Theophilus, styles John equally with the prophets as πνευματοφόρος, and asserts that both are equally inspired by the Holy Spirit, which moves their souls as the player sweeps the strings of the lyre. Irenaeus states explicitly the verbal inspiration of the Old and New Testament; together they are perfect "because they have been dictated by the Word of God and His Spirit[2]."

The establishment of the equal authority of the Old and the New Testament was not accomplished without difficulty. It was first the New Testament, as we have seen, which had to win its place beside the Old; now the Old Testament had to be defended in order to maintain its position as an authority for Christians. Jesus said that He came not to destroy, but to fulfil, yet there were many things in the Old Testament which seemed to be absolutely contradicted in the New. To Marcion the prevailing spirit of the Old Testament seemed so alien to that of Christ's teaching as to drive him to the conclusion that the God of the Old Testament was a different God altogether— a harsh and cruel Ruler who had later been deposed by the Father whom Jesus taught. Other

[1] *E.g.* Ignatius applies γέγραπται to the Gospels as well as the Prophets.
[2] *Contra Haereses*, II, 28, 2.

Gnostics, feeling the same difficulty, were led to reject scripture altogether and to appeal to reason alone.

These, however, were solutions not accepted by the Church. The solution accepted is one which has exercised a profound influence ever since on the Christian attitude towards the Bible. As a way out of the difficulty the Church adopted the Philonic mode of interpretation—a solution inevitable where a mechanical view of inspiration prevails and in an age which has no conception of evolution. The learning of the Alexandrians was turned to the *allegorical* interpretation of scripture. For Clement the facts of the Old Testament became symbols[1]. Origen has a definite scheme of a "triple sense" in scripture—the somatic, the psychic and the pneumatic. This view is reasserted by Jerome—while Augustine is inclined to believe that every pious interpretation is a genuine sense intended by the Holy Spirit[2]. The principle goes down to the Middle Ages in the conception of the threefold sense, literal, "typical," and moral.

It was obvious, however, that in the allegorical method there was danger to authority, although its essentially unsound character could not at that time be recognised. If everyone were allowed to interpret in his own way there would be no end to heresies. So the principle was formulated that

[1] In accordance with the principle, "nothing is to be believed which is unworthy of God." *Strom.* vi, 15, col. 124.
[2] J. Tixeront, *Histoire des Dogmes*, ii, p. 359.

only the Church is competent to decide the meaning of scripture in so far as it affects doctrine. The criterion of truth in interpretation is the Rule of Faith.

We see then that the first two of our "sources of faith" have amalgamated in "the Bible," a fixed and verbally inspired book of reference, interpreted by the Church. We must now trace the development of the other source, Christian prophecy.

Prophecy had been revived in the person of John the Baptist; it was revived once more in the great burst of religious enthusiasm which accompanied the founding of the Church. "Speaking with tongues" and other phenomena of religious excitation seemed to guarantee that the Christian prophet was the mouthpiece of a mind not his own. The "ministry of enthusiasm" exercised by those who appeared to be in the closest contact with the divine, necessarily ranked above the "ministry of office." But as time went on prophecy declined. There were abuses: "false" prophets existed, who traded upon the confidence of Christian communities, and these brought discredit upon the whole order. But more than this, prophecy, as a personal and spasmodic gift, was inevitably displaced by the regular ministry of the Church. Not all churches found prophets in their midst—often they were dependent upon travelling prophets for their charismatic ministry. The "heavy work of holiness" (Zoroaster) fell upon the bishops and presbyters, so that it was they who became the representative officials of the Church.

Prophecy as an institution...was destined to pass away, leaving those of its functions which were vital to the church's well-being to be discharged as a rule by the settled ministry, which rose to its full height only on its rival's fall[1].

The results of the decay of prophecy are well illustrated in the history of the Montanist movement. The Montanists were Christians who had become painfully conscious of the pressure of ecclesiastical authority and custom[2], and who protested against it by an appeal to the authority of a revived prophecy. Montanus and his followers claimed to stand in direct succession with Agabus and the other Christian prophets mentioned in the New Testament. They were the subjects of unmistakable psychic phenomena, which they declared were the fulfilment of the Lord's promise to "send the Paraclete." Under the influence of this inspiration they produced new scriptures, which were to supplement and in some ways to supersede the old. Against the Montanist claims the Church declared that the idea that there could be new scriptures was inadmissible—the canon was closed, "the number of the prophets was complete[3]." The prophetic spirit did indeed

[1] *Encyclopaedia Biblica*, article 'Prophetic Literature,' col. 3887.

[2] Cp. Tertullian, "Christus veritatem se, non consuetudinem, cognominavit." *De Virg. Vel.* i.

[3] Muratorian Fragment.

still exist, but it was in the Church as a whole, not in the ecstatic utterances of individuals. Henceforward the "living voice of the church" takes the place of the voice of prophecy as the second "source of faith." But it is an authority of a different kind. "The Paraclete" had indeed been "put to flight[1]" if His work be defined as consisting in the revelation of new truth; for it is now limited to assistance in apprehending and appreciating old truth. The work of the Holy Spirit is from this time to be detected not in the inspiration of private men, but in the pronouncements of ecclesiastical authorities upon matters of faith. The issue is well put by Dr Kidd in his chapter on Montanism:

Montanism stood for the legitimacy of accretive developments. But the Church admitted explanatory development alone[2].

We saw how the Church could not allow the individual interpretation of the Bible, the original Revelation; we see now how she was forced to reject the claim to add to it. The "faith once delivered to the saints" is the Bible alone, and the Bible is interpreted by the Church.

We can now sum up the growth of the Catholic conception of Revelation. The living word of Jesus the Messiah and His inspired apostles becomes

[1] Praxeas was said by Tertullian to have done this by his denunciation of Montanism. *Adv. Praxean*, c. i.

[2] Kidd, *op. cit.* p. 293.

"fixed" in the canon of the New Testament, which with the Old Testament is regarded as the basic authority. The living word of the Christian prophets is replaced by the explanatory function of ecclesiastical authority, which elucidates and determines the meaning of scripture.

It is these two sources of faith that constitute the Christian Revelation.

CHAPTER II

Christianity and Philosophy

THE fully-elaborated conception of the content of Revelation was not reached until the end of the development which we have just traced. The idea of Revelation, however, was an essential feature of Christianity from the first. The new religion claimed the sole allegiance of its adherents, and could not be syncretised. It was not an inevitable product of the religious conditions of the time, but appeared to come directly from God. It seemed as if God wished an entirely new start to be made. This *disparate* character of Christianity raised a problem—Christianity was admittedly a fresh start, but did this mean that all the existing religious practice and speculation of the world was to be swept away? Were educated converts to Christianity to jettison all their culture when they became Christians? Such a sacrifice was clearly not necessary, for much pagan thought was eminently in accord with Christian ideals. But here was a fresh problem. How was the resemblance between Christian teaching and certain results of pagan thought to be explained? In order to answer these questions, the Church was compelled to explain its relation to "Philosophy."

The Mediterranean world was essentially an educated world. There were no national wars under the Pax Romana, and no national politics. The leisured class was a relatively large one, supported by the labour of slaves. There was a general diffusion of a homogeneous type of culture. The educational system had two divisions—the literary and the scientific. The first of these was the province of the rhetorician: it does not concern us. The second department contained mathematics and philosophy. Of these, mathematics was regarded as a propaedeutic study, so that *philosophy* may be said to represent the whole non-literary side of Graeco-Roman education.

"Philosophy," it is needless to say, means primarily the investigation of truth; but in the reflective and unoriginal age with which we are dealing it had come to mean study of the different systems which had already been formulated. Correspondingly, "philosopher" became the name of a class of professional teachers on the "modern side," so to speak, of the education of the time. The living interest of the age was ethics; but everyone was a dilettante in metaphysics, and everyone was acquainted with philosophical terminology.

It is important to notice this characteristic of the thought of the period. It is not a dominant *system* that is in possession of the field of thought, but rather an attitude of mind. Every new idea introduced to such a period will have to bear philosophical scrutiny. Philosophy is the mill for which every "new thing" will be grist.

It is plain what must be the task of the Christian apologist if he is to commend his religion to such an age: he must express it in philosophical terms. We may contrast the situation with that in our own day. At the present time there is no general interest in metaphysics: the dominant study is Science. Hence the modern apologist is required to point to *facts*. Upon these he may if he wishes build up a metaphysic of his own, but criticism will be directed towards his facts rather than his theories. The modern mind demands evidence that will bear scrutiny: the ancient enquirer wanted theories that would hold water.

Christianity spread first as a practical religion having a minimum of theory. This sufficed so long as its message was presented to such as could correctly be described in St Paul's words as "not many wise." But soon the new faith began to attract the attention of the educated classes. To commend it to these was part of the task of the Apologists.

Hermias, Tatian and Tertullian were inclined to despise philosophy[1], but they themselves directed philosophical arguments against the atheistic Epicurean system. Justin, on the other hand, had been a philosopher, and did not give

[1] Tixeront, *op. cit.* I, p. 231.

up philosophy when he became a Christian. For
him Christianity is a philosophy, the only tenable
philosophy[1]. It fulfils and reinforces the older
philosophies, demonstrating[2] what they had only
conjectured. Here Justin is faced with the problem
of the "resemblance" between Christianity and
philosophy; how is it to be explained? He has
two solutions. As against the suspicion that
Christianity might have plagiarised the doctrines
of Socrates or Plato, he reiterates the curious
hypothesis of Philo—that these philosophers had
borrowed from Moses. The second explanation
is less bizarre. The Logos[3], which was manifest
fully in Christ, and had inspired in former ages
the Jewish prophets, had also worked in the
philosophers. The "seed of the Logos" was
present in each of them and had enabled them
to arrive at partial truth in their work of
discovery and contemplation[4]. Justin now
makes the bold claim that all who have thus
"lived with the Logos" were Christians; and their
noble sentiments are the property of the Christian community[5]. Pagan mythology, on the other
hand, had been the work of a demon, and its

[1] ταύτην μόνον εὕρισκον φιλοσοφίαν ἀσφαλῆ τε καὶ σύμ-
φορον. Dial. viii, 1, 2.

[2] μετ᾽ ἀποδείξεως. I Apol. xx.

[3] A conception already current in *part* of the Church
through "the Ephesian Gospel."

[4] δι᾽ εὑρέσεως καὶ θεωρίας.

[5] Ὅσα οὖν παρὰ πᾶσι καλῶς εἴρηται ἡμῶν τῶν Χριστια-
νῶν ἐστι. I Apol. xlvi, 3, 4.

existence supplied another motive for a full Revelation. Long since abandoned for philosophy by educated people, it had lingered on to be given its death-blow by the founding of the Church.

Justin is a typical protagonist of what we may distinguish as the first period of the relations between Christianity and philosophy. Christianity seeks to commend itself to a world in which philosophy is dominant; yet its attitude is a confident one. The boldness of Justin is significant. He adopts no defensive attitude, but appropriates all that is best in pagan thought for Christianity. The position which he took up had also its effect upon the Church itself. By some Christians philosophy was regarded as a dangerous "modernism," a cause of disunion. When, therefore, Justin's principles were accepted it meant both that philosophy was becoming Christian and that Christianity was becoming philosophical. We thus reach the second stage, that in which Christianity and philosophy are equals. This is the position of the Christian Platonists of Alexandria, whom we must now consider.

For Clement philosophy is a source of faith equally with Christian teaching: he is "à la fois profondément chrétien et résolument philosophe[1]." Both philosophy and the Christian revelation come from God. The former, however, comes indirectly[2], being drawn partly from the

---

[1] Tixeront, *op. cit.* 1, p. 282.
[2] κατ' ἐπακολούθημα. *Strom.* 1, 5, col. 717.

Old Testament (as Justin had suggested) and partly from the indwelling Logos, the gift of God. Philosophy was all that mankind had had to depend on in the days before the full Revelation. But now this is changed; philosophy has done its work as the sole source of enlightenment. What then is its present rôle? Clement declares that it helps faith ($\pi\acute{\iota}\sigma\tau\iota\varsigma$) to transform itself into knowledge ($\gamma\nu\hat{\omega}\sigma\iota\varsigma$). It criticises the content of Revelation, and by working upon it constructs *theology*, "the divine science of Revelation." Besides this, it disciplines the mind.

Origen is less enthusiastic about philosophy than Clement, but he continues to regard it as a source of faith and to use its methods. Its results he considers meagre[1].

At this stage philosophy is still considered an independent source of faith, but it is in process of being reduced to a subordinate position. *It is now, still more markedly, a collection of methodological principles, rather than a system of thought having its own presuppositions.* It would seem as if it were less important now to assert the claim of Christianity to be a philosophy. Was this because the Christian dogmatic system was rapidly incorporating Greek modes of thought[2]? It may be so; but there is at any rate another hypothesis. Christianity was the only religious philosophy that was really alive; it was coming to be realised

[1] Tixeront, *op. cit.* 1, p. 302.
[2] Cp. E. Hatch, *Influence of Greek Ideas, passim.*

that the other systems were not serious competitors. But further, within the Church there had always been those, especially in the West, who had regarded philosophy with suspicion. This suspicion was reinforced when the connection between philosophy and heresy became apparent. The spirit of free enquiry was apt to militate against Church discipline. The results of the ancient philosophers might safely be claimed as the property of the Christians; the philosophic method might be used to construct a theology; but there was no guarantee that philosophy would be content with this. Thus Tertullian recognises that the human mind had been "prepared" for the gospel: many a pagan thinker had had "an essentially Christian soul" —Seneca for example had often been on the Christian side[1]. But Tertullian distrusts philosophy as the parent of heresy[2]. This distrust is echoed by other Latin theologians. To the Latin mind, with its practical disciplinary bent, philosophy was a good servant but a bad master.

We thus arrive at a third stage in the relation between philosophy and Christianity—that of the subservience of philosophy. This development was assisted by the Trinitarian and Christological controversies which now supervene.

[1] "Seneca saepe noster" (*de Anima*, 20); Tixeront, *op. cit.* I, p. 344.

[2] "Haereticorum patriarchae philosophi." *Adv. Hermog.* viii.

As these were controversies within the sphere of
Revelation itself, philosophy could act only in
its subordinate capacity, *i.e.* as a methodology.

By the time of Augustine philosophy has
become "Reason." According to him, both in the
sacred and in the profane spheres there are two
forces leading to knowledge, Authority and
Reason[1]. Even before the coming of Christ
there were these two guides in the religious
sphere, for what is now called the Christian
religion existed from the dawn of the human race,
though it was *called* Christianity only after Christ
had come in the flesh. With this full revelation,
however, Reason loses its position as an independent source of truth. Its importance lies in
its relation to faith. Augustine's theory of this
relationship is expressed in the famous phrase
"Intellege ut credas, crede ut intellegas[2]."
Reason must *precede* Faith in order to examine
the credentials of what is offered for acceptance;
it must *follow* Faith in order to elucidate and
expound the content of what is accepted.

This becomes the principle governing the
relations of philosophy and faith for the re-
mainder of the Patristic and for the beginning
of the succeeding period. It remains only to
notice a Greek Father of the seventh century.

[1] "Gemino pondere nos impelli ad discendum, auctorita-
tis et rationis" (*Contra Academicos*, III, 43); Tixeront, *op. cit.*
p. 357.
[2] *Sermo* XLIII, 9.

Leontius of Byzantium is very philosophical, but his philosophy is *Aristotelian*[1]. This change to Aristotelian categories marks the final subordination of philosophy to authority. Theology has become a *deductive* science requiring the service of a *critical* philosophy.

Looking back over the Patristic period we observe the gradual subjugation of philosophy by theology. This was foreshadowed from the very first. "Philosophy" was not a quest for truth but rather the study of philosophical systems— a general acquaintance with them. In the general eclecticism Christianity too became eclectic and chose out of the common stock those principles which best illustrated its teaching. The claim of Justin that Christianity was a "philosophy," "the only tenable philosophy," was a bold one, but it soon gained general acceptance. By adopting philosophical principles and constructing a dogmatic system to which assent was demanded of all Christians, the Church became in one of its aspects a philosophical school. Since it met with no serious opposition it became the most powerful of such schools. But its philosophy was of a peculiar kind; a philosophy restricted to the working out of the implications of an infallible Revelation. When once Christian dogma had been completely worked out on the basis of such a Revelation, the task of philosophy was in a sense ended. The period of the equality

[1] Tixeront, *op. cit.* III, p. 9.

of Christianity and philosophy came *before* the great controversies which were to decide the doctrine of God and the doctrine of Christ. When these controversies were over, the last word had been said. The only function that could be permitted to philosophy was that of Reason, *i.e.* the subordinate function of criticism.

CHAPTER III

Faith and Reason

DURING the Dark Ages of Western Europe the Church alone stood firm amidst the dissolution of every other institution. Only under her wing was any remnant of the ancient culture safe[1]. Thus it came to pass that in matters of intellect Authority occupied the field, and Reason, in the sense of independent enquiry, was entirely absent. Of Augustine's "double weight" only one half survived. Theology was the mode of medieval thought[2]: its problems were dealt with at first by application to Revelation alone.

The reintroduction of an independent source of authority was made by John Scotus Erigena, who translated the Neoplatonic treatises ascribed to Dionysius the Areopagite. Upon this basis Erigena built up a mystical system, a fusion of Christianity and Neoplatonism. He explained the relation between theology and philosophy:

[1] For a list of the surviving classical works, see *Encyclopaedia Britannica*, article 'Scholasticism.' They include translations of the *Categories* and *De Interpretatione* of Aristotle, and of the *Timaeus* of Plato.

[2] R. L. Poole, *Illustrations of the History of Medieval Thought and Learning*, p. 2. Prantl says that there was no philosophy in the Middle Ages, only Theology and Logic, *Encyclopaedia Britannica*, art. cit.

true philosophy and true theology are identical. Human Reason is divine and is therefore entitled to interpret Revelation. The Bible cannot err, but it is sometimes in need of elucidation by human Reason.

This principle expresses the fundamental assumption of the medieval mind all through its creative period[1]. The truth of Revelation is so firmly established that it is impossible that Reason should ever contradict it. If there is any apparent contradiction it is Reason which must be wrong and which must give way. There is nothing deliberately obscurantist in this attitude. The Church was the wise Mother and the attempts of Reason seemed the essays of a child.

The principle enunciated by Erigena is important for our purpose, but his system lies apart from the main stream of medieval thought : the stream of which he is the source runs parallel to the main stream. The characteristic thought of the Middle Ages begins not with mystical speculation but with a logical problem. A sentence of Porphyry's *Isagoge* gave rise to the central problem of the nature of Universals, the two most sharply opposed views concerning which were styled respectively Realism and Nominalism. It was the resultant controversy which produced Scholasticism.

Scholasticism is not a philosophical system but a method of treating facts, a science of

[1] Cp. C. R. S. Harris, *Duns Scotus*, 1, ch. ii.

deductive reasoning. It was not long before the new method was applied to Revelation. This produced Scholastic Theology, the main intellectual interest of the Middle Ages. Ancient secular literature being almost entirely lost, there was only scripture for the mills of Scholasticism to grind.

The first application of dialectic to Revelation [1] was made by Berengarius, and it aroused the same alarm which the philosophical treatment of Christianity had produced in some of the early Fathers. It seemed likely that once more philosophy would be the parent of heresy. But the situation was saved by the attack of the Realists upon the "quasi-nominalism" of Berengarius. It was then seen that not all dialectic was destructive of orthodoxy, and Realism became the orthodox philosophical position.

The relation of Reason, represented by the revived dialectic, to Revelation was further defined by Anselm. He reasserted one half of Augustine's two-fold principle in the maxim "Credo ut intellegam": Faith accepts Revelation, and Reason draws out its implications. Theology once more becomes systematic. Reason is set the task of explaining as far as possible the mysteries of faith: it must co-ordinate data, solve difficulties

[1] By Revelation in this period we mean the Bible as interpreted by Christian tradition. The age of the Councils is over, and the pronouncements of the "living voice" of the Church are now embodied in dogma.

and provide logical ammunition for use against the Infidel.

With Abelard there comes recognition of the existence not simply of a dialectical method but of a body of thought independent of dogma[1]. He has some knowledge of pagan philosophy and wishes to reconcile dogma with it. He is bolder than Anselm: his *Sic et Non* is designed to shew by a series of antinomies the necessity for a dialectical reconstruction of theology. Yet he will not go too far: "I do not wish so to be a philosopher as to rebel against Paul, or so to be an Aristotle as to be parted from Christ[2]."

It seemed to Bernard of Clairvaux that this very result was actually being produced by the extension of the field of Reason. Accordingly he takes up a sceptical attitude. Full knowledge, independent of Revelation, is impossible in this life—there is only opinion. Faith, which enables the mind to accept Revelation, is a matter of the heart and will.

Hugo of St Victor classifies the ways of knowing as: knowledge, the fullest way; faith, a lower kind of knowledge; and opinion. He further distinguishes two kinds of knowledge, sacred and

[1] His philosophy, like the Cartesian, begins with doubt: "'by doubting we are led to enquire: by enquiring we perceive the truth.' It is not that he doubts that the two roads of reason and authority must ultimately converge...." R. L. Poole, *op. cit.* p. 116.

[2] "Nolo sic esse philosophus ut recalcitrem Paulo; nolo sic esse Aristoteles ut secludar a Christo." *Epistola* xvii.

profane. In the former class he includes "theologia mundana" or natural theology.

So far we have been dealing with a mere dialectic, or at most a philosophy thoroughly impregnated with dogma. But the recognition of a "theologia mundana" is the indication of a new stage in Scholastic thought. Up till now Reason has been in the plainest sense the "ancilla fidei." It is now becoming emancipated. And this movement is given a tremendous impulse by the discovery of a great body of independent thought, not a dialectical system but a scientific system—the works of Aristotle[1]. These produced a profound change in medieval theology.

The work of Aristotle is not exclusively nor even primarily theological, but theology being the preoccupation of medieval thought, the new principles were at once applied to the elucidation of the problem with which dialectic was dealing. But Aristotelianism refused to be degraded to a dialectical machine. Its conclusions were reached

---

[1] "These writings contained the text of the *Organon*, the *Physics*, the *Metaphysics*, the *Ethics*, the *de Anima*, the *Parva Naturalia* and a large number of other treatises of Aristotle, accompanied by continuous commentaries. There arrived besides by the same channel the glosses of Theophrastus, of Simplicius, of Alexander, of Aphrodisias, of Philoponus, annotated in the same sense by the same hands. This was the rich but dangerous present made by the Mussulman school to the Christian." Hauréau, 1, p. 382, in *Encyclopaedia Britannica, art. cit.* These works were translated from the Arabic through the Castilian into Latin.

by an entirely different method from the deductive treatment of texts. They did not demand faith in certain dogmatic presuppositions as an indispensable preliminary. How were the two systems—the one founded on authority, the other on reason—to be reconciled? The works of Aristotle could not be condemned wholesale, nor could the edifice of dogma be destroyed. There was only one solution: the spheres of Revelation (*sacra doctrina*) and of philosophy (*disciplinae philosophicae*) must be delimited, and the two studies regarded as independent ways of approach to the same subject.

It was impossible that a solution on these lines should ever be successfully attained. The two modes of knowledge could not, in the nature of things, keep their limits. Besides the inherent impossibility of fusion of the two systems, there was another cause tending to produce a divergence[1]. So far, the accepted theory of knowledge had been Augustinian or Neoplatonic—in every act of knowledge was present the light of the Increate Word. Thus a sharp separation between Natural and Revealed knowledge was impossible. But the new non-mystical Aristotelian epistemology rendered such a separation inevitable.

The change took place gradually. Thus Bonaventura attempts to reconcile Augustine and Aristotle, but his attitude remains Augustinian: "Nisi credideritis non intellegetis." Knowledge

[1] Harris, *op. cit.* p. 66.

comes through a gift of illumination vouchsafed to the eye of faith, which makes mysteries plain ; even heathen philosophers had a share of this faith. So long as this attitude remains there is no question of a sharp delimitation of spheres, one containing knowledge supernaturally imparted and the other confined strictly to the unaided efforts of the human Reason.

It is in Albertus Magnus that the separation definitely takes place[1]. Faith contains truths incapable of proof. The product of supernatural illumination, it supplies supernatural knowledge. Natural knowledge, on the other hand, is self-evidencing. Both are concerned with the same object but in entirely different ways[2].

Revelation thus regained that freedom from the criticism of logic whose disappearance Bernard of Clairvaux had once watched with such dismay. Earlier theologians had assumed that the mysteries of faith had rational basis to which it was possible to penetrate. This assumption was abandoned by Albert. After him, theology is regarded as consisting of a number of dogmas of which half are demonstrable and half the objects of faith.

It was Thomas Aquinas who stated fully this

[1] Albert was "the first Scholastic who reproduced the whole philosophy of Aristotle in systematic order with constant reference to the Arabic commentators and who remodelled it to meet the requirements of ecclesiastical dogma" (Ueberweg), *Encyclopaedia Britannica, art. cit.*

[2] Harris, *op. cit.* p. 69.

"Scholastic Synthesis"[1] and worked out its implications. Of particular importance for us is his treatment of the problem of the *relation* between the two spheres. Both led to truth; in both God was giving illumination. Why were there two illuminations, and in what respects did they differ?

To the first question Aquinas replies that in the first place man is ordained by God to an end which exceeds the comprehension of Reason. Yet this end must be known in order that man may direct his steps towards it. But further, even within the sphere where Reason is competent, instruction by divine Revelation is necessary, because

the truth about God, if sought by Reason alone would be forthcoming only for a few men, during a long period of time and mixed with many errors[2].

Yet all human salvation depends upon knowledge of this truth, which has accordingly been graciously revealed by God and must be received by Faith.

To the question in what respect the two sources of knowledge differ, Aquinas makes the same reply as Albert: that their diversity is due to the diverse modes of procedure employed[3]. For example, the astrologer and the physicist

[1] A term used by M. de Wulf, *Histoire de la Philosophie Médiévale.*

[2] *Summa Theologiae,* 1, i, 1.

[3] *Ibid.* "diversa ratio cognoscibilis diversitatem scientiarum inducit."

reach the same conclusion, *e.g.* that the earth is round, but the astrologer proceeds "mathematically and abstractly," while the physicist proceeds by a method which takes into account the material. In the same way, that branch of theology which deals with Revelation differs in kind from "natural" theology, although both have the same end, *i.e.* to discover the truth about God.

Aquinas recognised that even in the region where Reason was competent there might be antinomies: *e.g.* it is equally possible to maintain, as Kant has shewn, that the world is eternal and that it is not eternal. In these cases Revelation must decide. But Aquinas went further than this. He recognised that a proposition might commend itself to Reason, yet be contrary to Revelation. Here, again, Revelation must decide, for it is infallible, while Reason can err[1].

It is obvious that the position of the Scholastic Synthesis was unstable if it could lead to a conclusion like this. After Aquinas it begins to break down, and medieval thought enters a third period. Duns Scotus enlarged still more the sphere of authority. For him few doctrines are rationally demonstrable, for they are founded on the arbitrary will of God, who has revealed them to serve as guides for moral action[2]. Man must know

[1] The certitude of theology proceeds "from the light of the divine knowledge which can never be deceptive." Harris, *op. cit.* p. 75.

[2] This is the orthodox estimate of Duns Scotus' position;

what his true ends are and how they are to be achieved. The competence of Reason is partial—it deals with its object only so far as this can be grasped by a finite mind. William of Occam goes still further and denies that *any* doctrines are rationally demonstrable. Thus more and more doctrines are drawn under the shelter of Revelation[1], the competence of Reason is more and more denied, and the result is scepticism. It is as yet a scepticism in the philosophical though not in the popular and religious sense, for the presupposition of medieval thought still holds: it is impossible that Revelation should err.

Scepticism in the popular sense supervenes when the doubt becomes felt whether what is taught by the Church to be Revelation is actually true Revelation. This doubt is raised at the Renaissance, when the New Learning acts as a solvent upon the fabric of Revelation as defined by the Church. The result is the breaking of the union of Scripture and Tradition achieved in the Patristic Age, and the establishment of Scripture as the sole content of Revelation.

Looking back upon the medieval period we can see that it opens with the Church as the only surviving institution and with most pagan literature lost, so that the inspired literature of the

but contrast Harris, who thinks he has been unjustly treated on this point.

[1] Harris, *op. cit.* p. 75.

Church appears as something absolute, without relations. We were able to distinguish subsequently three stages of thought. The first is the growth of Reason as a dialectical instrument for the elucidation of Revelation. In the second stage we saw that the independent system of Aristotle could not be assimilated and was therefore joined on to Revelation as an equal authority, sharing with Revelation the territory of thought. Finally, in a third stage, this synthesis decays; the doctrine of double truth leads to scepticism; Revealed Theology attempts to justify itself as a *practical* science; but the inherent contradiction puts too great a strain upon the fundamental presupposition of the infallibility of Revelation, so that complete religious scepticism results.

The next period of our study will witness the establishment of the sole authority of Reason.

CHAPTER IV

Natural and Revealed Religion

THE effect of the New Learning in the sphere of religion was the Reformation, "the German Renaissance." The revived study of Greek threw a general doubt upon the accuracy of the Church's interpretation of Scripture, and this lent intellectual support to the revolt which other causes had combined to make inevitable. The Bible alone, without accretions, now constituted Revelation[1]. But the Bible pure and simple was not destined to remain the Reformers' guide of faith. There was no time for a suspense of judgment until accurate scholarship should arrive at a scientific method of interpretation. Indeed, the impartiality of scholarship was at a discount. The times demanded "slogans" and party cries; and the reformers found their watchword in "justification by faith alone." The Scriptures, which Calvin had declared "shone by their own light," came to be interpreted in the light of a new dogmatic position.

[1] Cp. the First Helvetic Confession, *Article* 1: "Scriptura canonica, verbum Dei, Spiritu Sancto tradita, et per prophetas apostolosque mundo proposita, omnium perfectissima et antiquissima philosophia, pietatem omnem, omnem vitae rationem sola perfecte continet." Our own Sixth Article is more negative.

In England, the country with which we must now concern ourselves, over a century was spent in the attempt to find a new authority which should be the guardian and licensed interpreter of Revelation[1]. The aim of the English reformers was to retain the old organisation, in a purified church without a foreign head. The Laudian divines worked out the implications of this position and tried to set up a new church-authority—that of the National Church. But this theory did not win general acceptance. It was opposed by the Puritan movement, at first in the form of Presbyterianism and later in that of Independency. The Presbyterians abandoned all ecclesiastical tradition and wished to return to what they conceived to have been the primitive state of the Church. Presbyterianism was followed by Independency, as Mark Pattison points out, as

its natural and necessary development. It was a consequence of the controversy with the establishment. For both the Church and Dissent agreed in acknowledging Scripture as their foundation, and the controversy turned upon the interpreter of scripture[2].

Both parties claimed as correct their own interpretation; the result was endless controversy; and this led to the seeking of new authority.

[1] Mark Pattison has very concisely summarised the stages of this quest. *Tendencies of Religious Thought in England, 1688–1750*, in *Essays and Reviews*, 12th ed. p. 396.

[2] *Ibid.* p. 351.

This new authority was discovered by the Independents and the Quakers in "the inner light." But the result of this discovery was still more controversy. What was wanted was some common authority to which all might appeal—not an external authority nor one accessible only to specially gifted natures. Such a new authority was found in Reason.

What Reason meant to the men of this time is explained by Pattison to be

Common Reason carefully distinguished from recondite learning, and not based on metaphysical assumptions [1].

This is only partly true, for the theologians of the time were unconsciously influenced by certain assumptions. The conception of a Natural Religion, the growth of which we are now to trace, owed its formulation to *philosophers*, who were necessarily influenced as much by previous speculation as by the "common reason" of their time.

At the Renaissance Philosophy had reappeared as the adversary of its degenerate offspring the scholastic dialectic. It endeavoured to free itself entirely from presuppositions and especially from religious assumptions. "Credo ut intellegam" gave place to the new principle that doubt is the beginning of knowledge. Henceforth Reason alone was to be the authority in the world of

[1] *Ibid.* p. 397.

thought. Philosophy would pursue her task without reference to Revelation, though her results might admit of an external reconciliation with it.

The revolution in thought inaugurated by Descartes was effected by the application in the sphere of philosophy of the principles which underlay the scientific triumphs of the Renaissance[1]. The criterion of the truth of an idea was henceforward to be its "clearness and distinctness," just as susceptibility of mathematical treatment had come to be that which marked off the "primary" from the "secondary qualities" of an object. It followed that also in the case of a complex idea like a religion the most real part of it was taken to be its dogmatic formulation; for this alone admitted of clear expression. It was regarded as the core of the system, though to it there attached themselves certain emotions and volitional states, in the same way as the secondary qualities of an object were thought to attach themselves to the primary. The concept, in short, was regarded as the substance, the volitional and emotional element as the shadow. It is this fundamentally rationalistic point of view that determined the course of the religious thought of the age. It is this that shaped the characteristic conception of a "Religion of Nature."

[1] Cp. E. A. Burtt, *The Metaphysical Foundations of Modern Physical Science*, Chap. iv.

The medieval unity of Christendom had broken up, and Europe was filled with jarring sects. For this condition of things the extermination of heretics was no longer a feasible cure, since orthodox and heretics were so equally balanced in number that the very conception of heresy took on a purely relative significance. It was obvious that all the sects could not be right in all their teaching, and the balance of probability was against any one being right and all the rest entirely wrong. That doctrine alone could be true which was *common* to all the sects. The true Christianity was a residual body of doctrine. But the argument did not stop here. The boundaries of the known world had lately been enormously extended, and whole civilisations, each with its characteristic form of religion, had been discovered [1]. The old conception of the world as consisting of a Christendom surrounded by a fringe of heathenism was no longer tenable. Instead, the world presented to the rational observer the appearance of a commonwealth of religious systems. Accordingly a further abstraction was made. The true religion must be one composed of the dogmas common to all existing religions. The doctrines thus left after the paring away of all differences constituted the Religion of Nature.

The Religion of Nature was believed to be

[1] The Chinese especially impressed the imagination of the time. Leslie Stephen calls them "the pets of the Deists."

the one to which the "faculty of reason which God hath implanted in mankind" was everywhere capable of attaining. By means of this faculty men were

capable of discovering at first the being and perfections of God and that He governs the world with absolute equity, wisdom, and goodness, and what duties they owe to Him and one another[1].

This view—that Reason, which one writer (Warburton) identifies exclusively with the quality in virtue of which man is in the image of God[2], leads inevitably to Natural Religion—was shared by all thinkers : "that stage theologians of all parties travelled in company." But now a division began to appear. One party (the Deists) felt that Natural Religion was sufficient; the other party was committed to a belief in Revealed Religion.

The former found that the light of reason which had guided them so far indicated no road beyond. The Christian writers declared that the same natural process enabled them to recognise the truth of Revealed Religion. The sufficiency of Natural Religion thus became the turning point of the dispute[3].

The early Deists were not concerned, or did not dare, to attack Christianity. They merely

[1] James Foster (1731) quoted by M. Pattison, *Essays and Reviews*, 12th ed. p. 324.

[2] *Ibid.*

[3] *Ibid.* p. 324. Note the essence of religious life defined as moral action.

assailed its character as a Revealed Religion, and tried to shew that it was essentially identical with the Religion of Nature. Its original state had suffered corruption and received accretions of irrelevant mystery. It was to prove this thesis that John Toland wrote his book *Christianity not Mysterious*. Another line of approach was taken by Matthew Tindal. The Deists had committed the mistake, to which as Rationalists[1] they fell an easy prey, of conceiving their system of evaporated dogma as having actually had historical existence as the primitive religion of the world. It was an illusion possible only to an age completely lacking in historical sense. The Rationalists pictured the universe as a *scheme*, where we figure it as a *process*; their archetypical science was geometry, where ours is history. It was natural that they should regard diverse systems of dogmatic propositions (which for them represented the essence of the different religions of the world) as derived from a few fundamental axioms : an age that possesses no historical sense can explain development only by logical derivation. Tindal's view is sufficiently expressed by the title of his book, *Christianity as Old as the Creation, or Christianity a Republication of the Religion of Nature*. The Religion of Nature had by the time of Christ become corrupt, and the

[1] Cp. C.C. J.Webb, *Problems in the Relation of God and Man*, p. 69. "By Rationalism I understand not belief in *reason*, but an exclusive reliance upon *reasoning*."

task of Christ had been to restore its primitive purity.

The orthodox, on the other hand, had to defend Christianity as a Revealed Religion, *i.e.* as something added to the Religion of Nature. It is the same problem as that which had confronted Aquinas in regard to the relation between natural and revealed theology, except that here two *religions* are opposed. The first answer of the apologists was, once more, that a revelation gives fuller information, which Reason could only painfully have acquired. Their second answer contains a significant difference from that of Aquinas. He had argued that man required knowledge of his end in order to be able to aim at it; the Rationalists argued that morality required revealed *sanctions* to compel men to be moral. It is Locke who enunciates the underlying principle:

Reason is natural revelation, whereby the eternal Father of light and Fountain of all knowledge communicates to mankind that portion of truth which he has laid within the reach of their natural faculties; revelation is natural reason enlarged by a new set of discoveries communicated by God immediately, which reason vouches the truth of, by the testimony and proofs it gives that they come from God.

Thus Reason is the judge of Revelation.

So that he that takes away reason to make way for revelation, puts out the light of both, and does much-what the same as if he would persuade a man to put out his eyes the better to receive the remote light of an invisible star by a telescope[1].

This quotation indicates the next step in the argument for Revelation. The antecedent probability of a Revelation being established, the controversy moves on to the question whether the alleged Revelation is indeed a true one, and this involves the submitting to the examination of Reason of "testimony and proof." The opponents of Revelation brought forward a varied array of argument: the incredibility of miracles, the inconsistencies of the Bible, the apparent immoralities of the Old Testament, the partial character of the alleged Revelation. It is against arguments of this kind that Butler's *Analogy* was written. After first urging that we must take Revelation as it is, without forming *a priori* theories as to what it ought to be, he endeavours to shew that it contains no greater difficulties than can be urged against the interpretation of "the constitution and course of nature" upon which Natural Religion is based.

When Deism, both of this and of the earlier type, began with surprising suddenness to die— it cannot be, remarks Leslie Stephen, because of the ability of its opponents—both the antecedent probability of a Revelation and the fitness of the Bible to be its embodiment had become generally accepted. It remained to shew that the alleged

[1] *Essay on the Human Understanding*, Bk iv, Chap. xix, Section 4.

historical facts which guaranteed Revelation were true.

The type of literature which undertook this task is wittily described by Mark Pattison as

that Old Bailey theology, in which, to use Johnson's illustration, the Apostles are being tried once a week for the capital crime of forgery[1].

This was not only the spirit, but in one case at least actually the form of apologetic. Sherlock's *Trial of the Witnesses* is a dialogue with a law-court as the scene. The conclusion of the "trial" is quoted by Pattison:

Judge—What say you? Are the Apostles guilty of giving false evidence in the case of the resurrection of Jesus, or not guilty? *Foreman*—Not guilty[2].

The famous *Evidences* of Paley is a kind of *Summa* of Rationalistic apologetic. Written in 1794, it is of course chiefly concerned with the "External Evidences," but the latter part of the book is devoted to "Auxiliary Evidences" and "Objections."

Paley begins with a short demonstration of two fundamental principles, (1) that a Revelation cannot be made in any other way except by miracles, and (2) that once we believe in God, miracles are not incredible. This preliminary discussion disposes of the general problem which had agitated the Deists and their opponents, and clears the way for the "evidences." These are

[1] *Essays and Reviews*, 12th ed. p. 314.   [2] *Ibid.* p. 366.

marshalled to prove two propositions, one positive and one negative. The first is

That there is satisfactory evidence that many, professing to be original witnesses of the Christian miracles, passed their lives in labours, dangers, and sufferings, voluntarily undergone in attestation of the accounts which they delivered, and solely in consequence of their belief in those accounts; and that they also submitted, from the same motives, to new rules of conduct.

The second proposition asserts that no other miracles (*e.g.* those of Mahomet) are similarly attested. The argument proceeds thus: first the fact of the sufferings undergone for the sake of a "story" is proved, then that this story is a miraculous one, and finally that it is identical with our New Testament.

The second part of the book, which deals with the "auxiliary evidences of Christianity," consists of a selection of "internal evidences" such as had occupied the previous age, now reduced to a subordinate place. The subjects discussed can be gathered from the chapter-headings: Prophecy, The Morality of the Gospel, The Candour of the Writers of the New Testament, The Identity of Christ's Character, the Originality of Christ's Character, The Conformity of the Facts occasionally mentioned or referred to in Scripture with the State of Things in these Times as represented by Foreign and Independent Accounts, Undesigned Coincidences, Of the History of the Resurrection, Of the Propagation

of Christianity. The third and final section of
the book is "A Brief Consideration of some
Popular Objections." The chapters are headed :
The Discrepancies between the several Gospels,
Erroneous Opinions imputed to the Apostles,
The Connection of Christianity with the Jewish
History, Rejections of Christianity, That the
Christian Miracles are not recited, or appealed to,
by early Christian writers themselves, so fully
or frequently as might have been expected,
Want of Universality in the Knowledge and
Reception of Christianity and of Greater Clear-
ness in the Evidence, The Supposed Effects of
Christianity.

We are now in a position to understand the
peculiar terminology of Mr Hulse. He wishes
to provide for all the departments of apologetic
which appear in Paley's book—(1) Direct Evidence, (2) Auxiliary Evidence and (3) Reply to
Objections. Thus, the Hulsean Lectures are to
exhibit "the evidence for Revealed Religion and
to demonstrate in the most convincing and persuasive manner the truth and excellence of
Christianity." The means by which this demonstration is to be effected are subsequently stated
to be "the proofs, especially the collateral arguments." By "proofs" here are plainly meant
"external evidences"—the "direct historical
evidences" of Paley's first Part; whilst the
"collateral arguments" clearly correspond to

the "auxiliary evidences" of Part Two. The former class may be said to deal particularly with the "truth" of Christianity, the latter with its "excellence." The rules for the Hulsean Dissertation are of the same scope. Finally, the "Christian Advocate" is to discharge the office of Paley in his third Part and "to prepare some proper and judicious answer to all such new and popular or other cavils and objections against the Christian or Revealed Religion[1]." Hulse further adds "or against the religion of Nature."

We must now examine the content and value of this view of Revealed Religion.

[1] For an extended application of the principle which equated "Revealed Religion" and Christianity, cp. Parson Thwackum in Fielding's *Tom Jones*: "When I mention religion, I mean the Christian religion; and not only the Christian Religion but the Protestant religion; and not only the Protestant religion, but the Church of England." Quoted by J. S. Huxley, *Religion without Revelation*, p. 176.

CHAPTER V

Critique of the Classical Theory of Revelation

THE word *revelation* denotes in the first instance an *act*; in religion, "God's making known His will." The different meanings attached to Revelation in the history of the Church are the result of different ideas of *how* such knowledge is imparted. When St Paul wrote that he knew certain things "by revelation," he meant that he knew them through a consciousness that God was speaking directly to him. The Alexandrian Fathers found the voice of God in scripture and philosophy. But after the period of the equal authority of Revelation and philosophy with which these Fathers are associated there began to grow up a distinction: the mind came to be thought of as entirely passive in the sphere of Revelation; but active in that of Reason. Both Reason and Revelation however were recognised as channels of communication with God. The Dark Ages almost extinguished the creative activity of the human mind, so that the passive channel of knowledge was left supreme. The voice of God was thought to be accessible only in "the living voice of the Church," the guardian of both scripture and tradition. With the revival of thought in the Middle Ages Reason began to take its place once more as a "source of faith": there were now two sources—Reason and Faith. At the Reformation the Reformers disallowed the claim of dogma to represent the voice of God, and scripture stood alone as the vehicle of Revelation. Revelation meant for them "the faith once delivered to the saints," and as such was identified with scripture, the "commandment of God" purged from the "tradition of men[1]."

Scripture had now lost its infallible interpreter, and the new interpretations, not being based on any fixed principle, were legion. A new interpreter was at length finally found in "common Reason." The Rationalists accepted the idea of Revelation as a body of truths once and for all fixed[2]—when the active exercise of the mind had done all it could, passive reception of truth was required to crown its efforts. Revealed Religion, based upon Revelation (*i.e.* the Bible), was the completion of Natural Religion, based upon the unaided activity of the human reason. This was the Rationalistic synthesis. But there is an important difference between this synthesis and that attained by the Scholastics. Revelation

[1] For the transition from Revelation as a process to Revelation as an object, cp. "sensation" = primarily "sensatio," secondarily "sensum."

[2] It is difficult to fix the *exact* connotation of "Revelation" at this period: for Paley and the theologians it plainly means "the truths enunciated by Christ"; but for the people at large it means, as plainly, the whole Bible.

was not accepted by the Rationalists as a matter of faith; it was regarded as verifiable by Reason[1]. Reason was employed first to determine the antecedent credibility of a Revelation and secondly to determine the credentials of the Revelation alleged. By the time of Paley and Hulse, the former of these enquiries had taken a subordinate place, and the latter almost exclusively engaged the attention of theologians. We must now examine the evidential "proof" of Revelation from the point of view of the modern *Weltanschauung*. But first we must very briefly indicate the movements of thought which have gone to make up the modern religious view of the world.

In summing up the characteristics of the two periods of eighteenth-century theology, Mark Pattison says:

The preceding age had eliminated the religious experience, the Georgian had lost besides the power of using the speculative reason[2].

With the decline of the "evidential" school of theology came the rebirth of these two activities.

The Methodist Revival had, before the end of the eighteenth century, leavened both the Church and Nonconformity. There was a general reaction against legalism; and the new attitude

[1] Butler: "Reason can, and it ought to judge, not only of the meaning, but also of the morality and evidence of revelation." *The Light of Nature*, p. 136.

[2] *Essays and Reviews*, p. 315.

gave rise to a new treatment of biblical exegesis, dogmatic theology, and Christian morals. The Bible was interpreted anew in the light of the experience of conversion, and was found to contain a "scheme of salvation." Instead of the "theology of attack and defence" the public demanded "gospel"; while Christian morality was commended not by arguments of prudence[1] but as the expression of a "saved" soul. In this atmosphere, the detachment necessary for weighing "evidences" was as out of place as the former cool and calculating morality.

The return to religious experience in Methodism, Evangelicalism, and Pietism was only part of a wider movement which also produced Romanticism in art and Nature-mysticism amongst those not attached to any Church. Upon this mysticism was built up the "philosophy of feeling" represented in Germany by Schleiermacher and Friedrich Schlegel[2], and in England by Coleridge.

This was the positive attack on Rationalism. The destructive work was done by Kant, who subjected the assumptions of Rationalism to a thorough criticism and concluded by denying the competence of theoretical reason in the "transcendent" sphere. Only through the Practical

[1] For Lord Chesterfield Christianity had been "a collateral security for morality."

[2] Goethe is not usually reckoned among the Romantics but cp. the famous line "Gefühl ist alles," *Faust,* 1. 3456.

Reason was there a sure pathway to ultimate reality. Pure Reason could attain certainty only in the phenomenal world.

The Kantian limitation of knowledge set free science from metaphysics [1], and provided further theoretical justification for a new scientific method which was growing up. The collapse of Rationalism turned men towards *facts*. Science no longer conceived itself bound to work out its theories to their metaphysical conclusion—it set itself to the humbler task of collecting, collating, and interpreting phenomena. The Baconian "inductive philosophy" had turned men's thoughts to practical science two centuries before, but it was only now that theoretical science secured its emancipation from metaphysics.

It remained, however, to find a principle of arrangement for the ordering of the increased accumulations of scientific data. This was found in the principle of continuity. This principle had indeed been asserted by Leibniz as a generalised application of his discoveries in the calculus; but lack of data had made it incapable of experimental verification [2]. But the *loi de continuité* was not self-explanatory—there was required a new principle of development. It had been a characteristic of Rationalism to regard reality as static, and in this

[1] The old term for Natural Science in the Universities was Natural Philosophy.

[2] Kant and Herder hazarded guesses about the evolution of life from "crystals" up to man.

respect Kant was still a Rationalist[1]. But there had been growing up a *dynamic* view of the world. The renewed interest in life as distinct from logic had led to a revived study of history, and this led in turn to a new application of the principle of causality. The explanation of a given phenomenon began to be sought in its *antecedent*—it was regarded as the *development* of its antecedent. The principle of continuity arranged the facts, the principle of development interpreted this arrangement[2].

The new principle revolutionised one science after another. In Geology "the testimony of the rocks" led irresistibly to the conclusion that the creation of the world had been a process, not an instantaneous act. In Biology the new principle, applied to an accumulation of facts such as had been available to neither "Moses" nor Aristotle, made the inference inevitable that man was descended from a lower type of animal.

These new scientific developments had a catastrophic effect upon the traditional view of the Bible. There seemed to be no escape from the dilemma, "*Either* science *or* the Bible is false." But it became no longer possible even to speak of the Bible as being "true," when scientific

[1] Cp. his conception of "architectonic," and his static, purely logical categories.

[2] *E.g.* the principle of continuity can arrange scientifically the facts of biology, but only the principle of development can make the assertion "ontogeny recapitulates phylogeny."

methods began to be applied to the Bible itself. It was shewn that scripture itself was the product of a process of development. The idea of its *perseity*, so to speak, was destroyed. This discovery, while it provided for those who accepted scientific conclusions a way of "saving" the Bible, dealt the final blow to the age-old view of the nature of scripture.

We may now proceed to the examination of the Paleyan apologetic.

I. The whole argument depends ultimately on *miracle*. To-day it is not necessary to believe in a "cast-iron" universe to have a predisposition against miracles. It is impossible to *exclude* them on scientific or philosophical grounds, but "probability is the guide of life" and it is improbable that miracles do occur: "Of laws which never shall be broken we know nothing"—"but of laws which never are broken we know a good deal[1]."

This is the modern *a priori* attitude towards miracles; there is a further argument against miracle as evidence.

In nature and from nature, by science and by reason we neither have nor can possibly have any evidence of a *Deity working miracles*;—for that we must go out of nature and beyond science[2]. If we could have such

---

[1] Statement made by F. R. Tennant in *Miracle*, with the comment of J. S. Bezzant; both quoted in H. D. A. Major, *English Modernism*, p. 131.

[2] This is in effect what Paley does, and so stultifies his argument. He commits a *petitio principii* by assuming the kind

evidence *from nature*, it could only prove extraordinary *natural* effects which would not be miracles in the old theological sense, as isolated, unrelated and uncaused; whereas no *physical* fact can be conceived as unique, or without analogy and relation to others, and to the whole system of natural causes[1].

It is useless to rest an argument upon a phenomenon which cannot be verified.

II. If we are to believe in the recorded "miracles" at all, it must be as an act of faith. But this will not allow us to restore miracles as the criterion of the truth of Revelation. We believe in miracles in this case as part of Revelation, not as a preliminary to its acceptance[2]. "Miracles are always *objects* not *evidences* of faith[3]." The reason for our faith must lie in something else, *e.g.* in the intrinsic excellence of the Revelation.

III. The miracles are thought to be authenticated by "testimony." The Paleyan school poses the dilemma: "*Either* the apostles were frauds *or* what they reported was fact": there is no

of God asserted by the revelation he is seeking to prove: cp. his question, "In what way can a revelation be made except by miracles?"

[1] Baden Powell, *Essays and Reviews*, 12th ed. p. 170.

[2] Cp. A. Sabatier, *Outlines of a Philosophy of Religion*, p. 279: "To base the value of religious notions on a supernatural authority with a view to rendering them indisputable is a vicious circle; the authority, it is evident, is the product of these notions themselves."

[3] *Essays and Reviews*, p. 171.

choice. To the modern mind the word "fact" begs the question. How can we be sure that the witnesses were not honestly mistaken? A reported fact is always a fact unconsciously interpreted by the witness's mind and affected by his presuppositions. If he is predisposed to accept marvels, he will report them. Paley is committing a rationalistic fallacy in recognising no mean between photographic accuracy and deliberate falsehood.

Thus the evidences fail; but how are we to regard Paley's conception of the nature of Revelation itself? It is a "positive external Divine revelation[1]." This is why it was thought to be capable of "proof" by evidence. It is a body of alleged fact, communicated under a divine guarantee, designed to inform us of "the future happiness of the good and the misery of the bad, which is all we want to be assured of[2]." Can we accept this view of the content of Revelation?

If there is any moral to be drawn from a survey of the relations between Reason and Revelation, it is that any information as to historical fact can be guaranteed by Reason alone. There can be no "double truth" in the same world of fact. If "Revelation" teaches that the world was created in six days, Reason will contradict it, and such a professed Revelation must be rejected.

It was inevitable that Revelation should be

[1] *Essays and Reviews*, p. 120.
[2] Paley's *Evidences*, ed. E. A. Litton, p. 361.

regarded as "positive and external" so long as certain conceptions obtained. Chief of these is the belief in the *final and closed* character of Revelation. The Middle Ages had had the living tradition of the Church, but the Reformation substituted the written word—the faith once delivered to the saints. It is interesting to notice a series of revolts against this conception. The Montanists, as we have noticed, protested against the closing of Revelation and its confinement to Scripture and the Church. The "voice" of the Catholic Church seemed less living than that of the prophets. They claimed that the same inspiration was present in themselves as had dictated the scriptures; and they produced new scriptures. At the Reformation Scripture was declared to be the sole authority, and also to be accessible to individual interpretation. So there occurred revolts against those who limited inspiration by the "Analogy of Scripture," and by national Church authority. The Anabaptists and the Quakers claimed new Revelations. This second revolt shared the fate of that of the Montanists, and Revelation was once more asserted to be closed and final. As a corollary to this, Revelation was regarded as *homogeneous* throughout: the result of the inspiration once given was a Bible equally inspired from cover to cover.

A second factor which supported the idea of a positive Revelation was the conception of its *purpose*. For Aquinas it supplemented the natural

Reason by giving man knowledge of the aim of his life and information as to how he should attain it. The aim of life was salvation, to attain Heaven and escape Hell. It followed that God, if He were good, must have provided the most explicit and detailed instructions as to how this was to be achieved. There must be a positive external Revelation—"sacra doctrina." This idea, again, was taken over, though in an altered form, by the Reformers: Heaven and Hell depended respectively on acceptance and rejection of "grace"; and knowledge of this clearly came by the Bible. The conception was further metamorphosed by the Rationalists. Heaven and Hell depended on good or bad living. But there was a difference in the conception of what this implied. The principles of morality were regarded as accessible to the unaided natural reason. The function of Revelation must therefore be to reveal not the *principles* but the *sanctions* of morality. On this view, as on the two former views, a positive external Revelation was necessary to serve as a guide-book to salvation.

The modern study of the Bible has destroyed the conception of Revelation as a body of *facts*. It is therefore no longer susceptible of external guarantee. Nor will modern ethical standards allow us to picture God as damning those who fail to accept an external authority. Revelation is no longer identified with the Bible.

The Bible is not so much a revelation as the *record*

of a revelation, and the inmost and most essential truths which it contains have happily been placed above the reach of Exegesis to injure, being written also in the Books of Nature and Experience and on the tables, which cannot be broken, of the heart of Man.

This sentence of Farrar's[1] indicates at once what must be the modern type of evidence—*internal* evidence—and also what must be its character.

It is interesting to note that even in the school of Paley there is a tendency to raise internal evidence from its place as auxiliary evidence and to make it the real test of Revelation.

Some of the most strenuous assertors of miracles have been foremost to disclaim the notion of their being the *sole certificate* of Divine communication, and have maintained that the true force of the Christian evidence lies in the *union* and *combination* of the *external* testimony of miracles with the *internal* excellence of the doctrine; thus in fact practically making *the latter the real test of the admissibility of the former*[2].

"Internal" evidence, indeed, has actually always been for the plain man the practical test of Revelation. It is not entirely the doctrine of verbal inspiration that has produced such extraordinary reverence for the text and letter of the Bible: it is rather the reverence which the spiritual content of the Bible has been able to inspire that has justified the theory of inspiration. "The Bible is capable of inspiring others because it is itself inspired." The "excellence" of much of its

[1] *A History of Interpretation*, p. xiv.
[2] Baden Powell, *Essays and Reviews*, p. 144.

contents has been such as to inspire a reverence which has spread (unwarrantably) to the whole, giving rise to the wildest allegorical treatment. The driest of genealogies has been regarded as susceptible of spiritual interpretation because of the unique value of the Prophets. If we to-day reject the theory of wholesale inspiration, that theory at least serves to shew that the Bible has in every age commended itself by its "internal evidence."

What then are the prolegomena to the modern discussion of Revealed Religion? We shall still define such a religion as one which is based upon divine revelation, yet that revelation will not be "positive" and capable of external attestation. It will not be, as heretofore, a book or a body of doctrines—these may *enshrine* it but they will not *constitute* it. We shall regard that book and these doctrines which have hitherto passed for Revelation as in a sense *Revelation at second hand*— the record of a Revelation made immediately to others, yet serving as a source of inspiration for ourselves. Finally, we shall suspect that the Revelation thus made to chosen men will not be *sui generis* and wholly different from anything we ourselves are capable of receiving. For if we can be inspired by Revelation at second hand, this must be because it appeals to a capacity which is latent in all of us.

In the next two chapters we shall discuss the form and content of Revelation in the light of modern theology.

PART TWO

CHAPTER VI

The Mode of Revelation

WE have seen the breakdown of the dualistic view of the relation of Natural and Revealed religion. We have now to notice a feature in the historical elaboration of this view which points the way to a truer theory.

In its most logical form the theory we have been considering would make Revelation something absolutely transcendent. Reason would make its discoveries up to a certain point, Revelation would then impart a set of ideas entirely disparate. But in point of fact there has never existed in history such a completely logical theory. It has always been realised that information as to the existence and attributes of God would be meaningless to a mind that was incapable of conceiving of the possibility of a God. It could have no possible significance for such a mind[1]. Accordingly, an entirely *sui generis* Revelation has

---

[1] Cp. Dr L. P. Jacks (in a lecture): "It would be like the principles of mathematics expounded to one's dog."

never been conceived: Reason has always been
allowed to attain to the conception of the character, and generally to some knowledge of the
nature, of those ideas which Revelation imparts.
We find this admission in all those periods of
"synthesis" which we have noticed. For Clement
philosophy is what the Law had been for St Paul,
"a tutor to bring us to Christ[1]," and he asserts
the right to judge Revelation in the statement,
"nothing is to be believed which is unworthy
of God." In Aquinas and Duns Scotus Reason
must attempt to mount up to Revelation, and
the truths of Revelation are such that they can
be defended by Reason. In Locke there is the
simile of the eye; Reason is the natural organ
whereby we perceive Revelation. Finally, in the
period following Locke the Deistic controversy
thrashes out all the possible relations there can be
between the two modes of knowledge: Revelation republishes, reinforces, reasserts, anticipates,
completes the discoveries of Reason[2]. We have
seen however that it has never been possible to
hold for long the balance between the two: Reason
has constantly tended to usurp the province of
Revelation, except indeed in the first period, when
philosophy was declining. It is clear that the distinction between Reason and Revelation, between

[1] παιδαγωγὸς εἰς Χριστόν. Gal. iii. 24.
[2] Besides this, a certain "revealed" character was not
denied to Natural Religion itself. Cp. Butler, Tindal, and
the Protestant dogmatic conception of "Revelatio naturalis."

Natural and Revealed Religion, can to-day no
longer be maintained.

Nor is there any need to continue to champion
this dualistic theory. So long as the notion of a
positive, external, *sui generis*, literally-inspired
"Revelation" held its ground, it was necessary
to conceive of God as communicating knowledge
of Himself in two ways, to attempt to justify these
two communications, and to harmonise their often
diverse data. To-day there is no such need. The
Bible is now seen to be not a collection of *Him-
melsbriefe*, but a literature in which are depicted
some of the most sublime strivings of the religious
spirit towards knowledge of God. Revelation has,
in effect, taken on that *active* sense which has
always belonged to Reason. The reception of
Revelation can no longer be regarded as the
merely passive acceptance of divine truth, for it
is seen to be a form of *knowledge*[1]. Revelation
remains God-given, but Reason becomes so too.

[1] It was the work of Kant to vindicate systematically the
active character of cognition, but the principle had been
enunciated already by the Cambridge Platonists. Thus
Cudworth (*Eternal and Immutable Morality*, iv, i) says:
"Knowledge is not a passion from anything outside the mind,
but an active exertion of the inward strength, vigour, and
power of the mind." Cp. A. Sabatier, *Outlines*, 278: "The
mind is a thinking and willing force, that is to say a force
productive of thoughts and volitions...We must affirm no
doubt that God creates this force and directs its evolution,
but it is a contradiction to say at once that He creates it and
that it is unproductive."

60

It is in a religious *quest* that Reason appropriates
the truth about Himself which is given by God.
The principle for which the old idea of *passiveness*
in Revelation unconsciously stood is the "given-
ness" or "thereness"[1] of religious truth. Discovery is the acquirement of knowledge by
mankind, Revelation the granting of that knowledge by God: both are the same process regarded
from different sides. Without God's will we can
obtain no knowledge of Him, nor indeed any
knowledge at all; but effort on our own part is
indispensable. There is a "mental initiative"[2] in
religious as in all other knowledge.

From this point onwards, then, we shall regard Revelation in this way, as the reverse side
of the religious quest: in trying to find out what
is the *form* of Revelation we shall proceed from
the human side, endeavouring to see in what ways
man has in history attempted to reach a knowledge
of the divine existence and essence. By working
thus we shall be heeding Butler's warning concerning "Our Incapacity of Judging, what were
to be expected in a Revelation." Then, having
found out the nature of the alleged discovery we
shall be in a position to ask whether it is a *true*
discovery and therefore "Revelation."

[1] The terms are von Hügel's, *Essays and Addresses*, II,
chap. ii.
[2] J. R. Illingworth, *Reason and Revelation*, note I, where he
quotes Cudworth, *loc. cit.*

In speaking of the attempt to discover, we pre-suppose *one who seeks* and *that which is sought*. In the case of the religious quest these are respectively Mankind and the Divine.

It is necessary to use the word "divine" instead of "God," because at the earliest stage of religion there is no conception of God or even of gods. The idea of a "primitive monotheism" is a fantasy which has no justification in the facts of anthropology or history. Religion begins with the feeling that sacredness or "the numinous" resides in certain objects, events or ideas[1].

Towards "numinous" objects[2] there are three possible attitudes—the affective, the volitional, and the cognitive. Primitive man is, for instance, full of *fear* of the numinous, and this is the root of worship. Again, he feels compelled to *do* certain things, *e.g.* to take steps to please the divine or to avert its wrath. Finally, he is compelled to *learn* the nature of the divine, in order to know what to do. These three attitudes cannot of course be kept separate. Magic is a science, and so belongs to the cognitive attitude, yet it is a *practical* science,

---

[1] J. S. Huxley, *Reason without Revelation*, p. 182 : "It is an entire mistake to conceive that the objects of this religious feeling are essentially or primitively of the nature of Gods. Some things, some events, some ideas are sacred, numinous, full of *mana* : that is all." This book, though not by a specialist in the subject, gives a good idea of the broad results of investigation into primitive religion.

[2] Using "object" in the widest sense.

designed to influence the divine for human purposes. Similarly, worship is not always the pure expression of religious awe, but also a necessity for propitiating the divine. We are not however here concerned with the affective and volitional attitudes, but must trace the development of the cognitive attitude—the quest for knowledge of the divine. This quest we find to have been conducted (i) in a practical and (ii) in a theoretical manner.

(i) On the practical side knowledge is sought by attempting to get special information from the divine power itself. This is *divination*. The behaviour of sacred objects is held to indicate the will of the power residing in them.

At a slightly later stage[1] in the evolution of religion, power is regarded not as residing actually *in* the numinous object, but as *behind* it. The behaviour of the object is still the index of a will, but of a will using the object as its tool. Divination therefore still continues; it is still employed to interpret the "voice" of the thunder, the flight of birds, the rustling of trees. It becomes a highly-elaborated "science." But a science demands specialists. Not all can divine, but only those who are specially gifted or who can devote time to study the science. Thus the expert, the *special person*, enters religion.

It is very important to notice this. The most primitive religion is, as far as can be conjectured,

[1] J. S. Huxley, *op. cit.* p. 244.

a private affair. Every man is in equal contact with the numinous. Without the offices of any specialist he detects, or thinks he detects, the divine in things, and he is his own priest[1] and his own magician. But religion does not remain at this stage. Experts must be set apart and supported by the labour of others: diviners to interpret "signs," priests to celebrate rites correctly, and magicians to perform magical practices in the most efficient way. We have here an actual distinction corresponding to the speculative distinction between Natural and Revealed religion. The first stage is the true Natural religion; when the expert comes in, there is Revealed religion[2].

(ii) The diviners, then, are the alleged "revealers" who attempt to ascertain, for *practical* purposes, the will of the divine powers. What is it that gives rise to the *theoretical* interest? The "science" of divination grows. At the same time there is growing up a sacerdotal system and a system of magic. These developments afford data upon which *reflection* is bound to take place. This reflection is the work

[1] "It is certain that originally every man was his own priest, and the ritual observed in later times by the priests is only a development of what was originally observed by all worshippers." W. Robertson Smith, *The Religion of the Semites*, p. 452.

[2] In the case of divination we may contrast *lot* as a form of divination with that performed by experts: the former is the mode in "natural," the latter in "revealed" religion.

of the theoretical side of the cognitive attitude. Its product is rationalisation in the form of "vague and fluid myths[1]." Divination is the attempt to ascertain the divine will by special means and for particular purposes. Mythology is the attempt of the primitive mind to explain to its own satisfaction the will and nature of the divine as it presents itself in all the traditions and practices of religion.

Nothing certain is known about the early growth of mythology, but here again we may suspect a personal factor—myths cannot grow of themselves. Each step in their elaboration must be the work of some one particular person, however obscurely his work can be traced. This fact too is important, for it shews that on the speculative side also, religion advances by the efforts of special persons.

Bearing in mind the lines of development we are attempting to follow—that of the cognitive attitude in religion, as manifested in (i) practical attempts at discovery, in divination, and (ii) theoretical attempts, in mythological speculation —let us attempt to trace further the growth of religion.

As we proceed further, the ground becomes firmer. We saw that in the later stages of primitive religion supernatural power came to be regarded as *behind* objects. The developed form of this belief is familiar in Greek polytheism.

[1] J. S. Huxley, *op. cit.* p. 243.

The divine powers have become personified, and a complicated mythology has grown up. There is evidence here of the truth of our conjecture that mythology has always been the work of special minds: Herodotus tells us that Homer and Hesiod formed the Greek theogony, "giving the gods their titles, distinguishing their particular duties and crafts, and indicating their personal appearances[1]." But the highly-elaborated "mytho-theology" of more or less independent gods was only another stage in religious development. The attempt to explain the divine nature by picture-thinking was opposed by the growth of rational thought. The result of this was criticism of the inconsistencies, both metaphysical and moral, of the mytho-theological scheme, leading finally to an ethical monotheism. This process accordingly forms a further stage in the evolution of religion.

With the arrival of universal or general ideas as dominant in religion there comes a change. The logical reason...pushes on to complete all possible conclusions from the premisses provided her. If Nature is a unity there are not many Gods but one God. If he is really God he is all-powerful, all-wise, and all-good...[2].

We can see these ideas at work in Greek literature. The moral critique of mythology was begun by Xenophanes and carried on by Plato and Euripides. The intellectual attack was the result of the rise of philosophy, which quickly

[1] Book II, 53.   [2] J. S. Huxley, *op. cit.* p. 247.

arrived at a theoretical monotheism. Both lines were fused later in the religious system of Stoicism, which took morality as its centre, and in its theology regarded the gods as manifestations of one divine principle.

The art of divination still went on during this speculative development. But it became a blind alley allowing no progress. Divination, it was realised by the enlightened, was based on a false conception of divine revelation—it was not by that means that the God of monotheism spoke to men. Thus the chief line of religious development in Greece ends in a *philosophical* religion devoid of religious experience, its mode of direct access to the divine having failed. Greek religious speculation did not succeed in "linking the intellectual side of belief with religion's central core of feeling[1]." Feeling was catered for along an entirely different line of development, in the Orphic and Mystery religions.

We must now turn to the history of a people among whom this unification was successfully effected. In *Israel* the channel of direct communication between the divine and human was kept open because it shared in the general development of religion and was indeed the actual *mode* of that development.

[1] A phrase used by J. S. Huxley in another connection (p. 245).

In Hebrew society, as in Greek, there was at first mythology on the one hand, and divination on the other. But from the diviners or "seers" emerged a new phenomenon—the "prophet." It is uncertain how this emergence took place. We are only told "he that is now called a Prophet was beforetime called a Seer[1]." It may however be considered to have occurred somewhat in this way: The divine power had always been thought to reside not only in objects, ideas, and events, but in some *persons*—the "possessed." Thus dervishes are still the objects of reverence in the East. In the possessed there must have seemed to be open a more direct channel of communication than was available through the rule-of-thumb methods of ordinary divination. Divination still went on, but there arose a type of seer who did not practise divination, being in his own person a mouthpiece of the divine[2].

The Hebrew prophet[3] was conscious of being filled with the divine inspiration: he heard the "word of Yahweh." The general purport of the divine message was regarded by the early

[1] 1 Samuel, ix, 9.

[2] For simultaneous use of both divination and prophecy, cp. the election of Saul, when both lot and consultation of Samuel were resorted to. Cp. Hastings' *Dictionary of the Bible*, article 'Prophecy.'

[3] In Greece προφήτης was the term for a particular type of *diviner*—one who interpreted and proclaimed the message of the frenzied Pythia.

prophets[1] as a call to establish Israel as a kingdom of Yahweh, a kingdom of righteousness. But the kingdom which was actually founded was from the first very far from the ideal as the prophets conceived it; so that the prophets began to declare that Yahweh had rejected Israel.

In the conflict of the prophets with the perversity of the kings and the waywardness of the people were hammered out ideas of unique religious importance: the idea of One God, the idea of that God as demanding justice, mercy, contrition, and as holding the individual as well as the nation accountable for sin.

Thus the Hebrew prophet is much more than the lineal descendant of the seer. As a diviner he reads the signs of the times and so detects the will of Yahweh towards his people; as a "possessed" man he is conscious of divine inspiration; as a reflecting man he points out the theoretical implications, both theological and moral, of what he sees. But first and foremost stands his character as a "God-intoxicated man." It is his inspiration that opens his eyes, mind and heart.

The prophet may be called a "revealer" in a sense that can be applied to no other religious "expert" we have so far considered. The diviner was on a false track; so, we may say, was the mythologist[2]. The philosopher and the moralist

[1] Samuel, Elijah, and Elisha.

[2] He was on the right track so long as picture-thinking was the only available mode of thought; but on the wrong

are on the right track, yet they are not interested primarily in religion. The prophet, on the contrary, "seeks first the Kingdom" and the rest is "added unto" him.

It is generally agreed that the religious education of the Hebrews was mainly the work of the prophets. Without them Israel would have remained at the same level as the surrounding nations. But it is not to Israel alone that we must look for prophets. All the "higher religions"—Islam, Buddhism, Christianity itself—have been founded by alleged prophets. But there is an important difference between these religions and that of the Hebrews. In an "historical" religion the personality of the founder is so important that he gives his name to the religion. He is not merely an important figure in the development of a religion but its very centre. In the case of Christianity and of Buddhism the founder is very definitely "more than a prophet"—He is an incarnation of the divine; He has for believers "the religious value of God[1]," "is felt to belong...to the side of the numen itself[2]." The significance of the outstanding position of these founders we shall discuss later; at present all we need notice is the enhanced importance of the prophet in the higher religions.

one in so far as mythology persisted after rational thought had been born.

[1] W. B. Selbie, *Schleiermacher*, p. 258.

[2] R. Otto, *op. cit.* p. 162.

What is the conclusion to which our discussion has led? It is that the development of religion is the work of special individuals[1]; that although this work can only with difficulty[2] be traced in the lower religions, in the higher it is so obvious that each of these religions is named after a man who is regarded as its *fons et origo*.

The thesis that Prophecy[3] is the mode of religious evolution is capable of verification only when a wide range of data from the field of comparative religion is available. Yet as a hypothesis it is not new. It was first put forward by Herder[4], one of the earliest philosophers to employ the modern historical method. Taking over from Lessing the conception of religious evolution as the "education of the human race," he proceeded to inquire how this evolution was brought about. He posits first of all a "natural revelation." This is conceived in accordance with the rationalistic ideas of the time as "present in man's reason and conscience,"

[1] The alternative theory is that it is the work of "the undifferentiated aggregate of individuals in mutual interplay." Otto characterises this view as "sheer fantasy," *op. cit.* p. 154 n.

[2] "The moments in which real notions of the nature and will of God dawned on the pious may be quite obscure in the memory of later generations." H. H. Wendt, *The Idea and Reality of Revelation*, p. 42.

[3] From this point we shall use "Prophet" (with a capital letter) in the widest sense, as equivalent to Revealer.

[4] 1744–1803.

not as a full-grown inherited idea, but as "the feeling
—which underlies all the ideas of the reason—for
the invisible in the visible, the one in the many, the
power in the effects[1]."

But this universal natural revelation was supplemented from the first by the personal influence of "remarkable original minds," those

guardian angels of our race, who with their minds
illumined the age in which they lived, who folded
nations to their hearts, and lifted them, even against
their will, to put forth giant power. They shine far
above the rest, like stars in the darkness of night.
They sacrificed their lives, just to be true to the word
and the deed which they bear in themselves as their
divine vocation[2].

This eloquent passage is a perfect description of
the Prophetic type of man: the only criticism
to be urged against it is that its rationalistic
outlook credits the diviner at the dawn of history
with the many-sided and developed virtues of
the Prophet.

The view that religious progress is the work
of geniuses is, after all, but an application of a
principle which has received the widest recognition: the principle that all progress is the
work of great minds. Thus Carlyle wrote:
"Great men are the inspired texts of that divine book of Revelations whereof a chapter is

[1] O. Pfleiderer, *The Philosophy of Religion* (Eng. trans.),
I, p. 218.
[2] Quoted, *Ibid.* pp. 218 f.

completed from epoch to epoch and by some named History[1]."

The form of religious evolution, then, is Prophecy; or rather the Prophet is the final stage in the series of those personalities who have sought knowledge of God. What is Prophecy? We may extract a provisional definition from our examination of its historical manifestations: Prophecy is the enunciation of religious principles by a person conscious of inspiration.

What is inspiration? This question we must now try to answer.

[1] *Sartor Resartus* (quoted by F. W. Farrar, *A History of Interpretation*, p. xiii). All "heroes" are here regarded as revealers of the divine even though their specific genius be not religious.

CHAPTER VII

Creative Inspiration

THE Prophetic experience may be analysed
into two "moments": the sense of communion[1] with the divine, and the sense of new
truth to be proclaimed. We must now examine
the nature of these moments.

But before we do so it is important to notice
that they are not extraordinary and unparal-
leled; they are not peculiar to the Prophet alone.
On the contrary, they are present in ordinary
religious experience. It is in virtue of the simi-
larity of the religious experience of the Prophet
and that of the ordinary Believer[2] that the
Prophet's message finds a hearing.

We saw that the idea of an absolutely
sui generis Revelation has seldom been enter-
tained in actual fact, since it allows no point of
contact between human and divine truth. Man
could not recognise the divine were there not
already present in his soul a "natural Revelation." Now Revelation is made through
Prophets. There must, therefore, be some capacity actual or latent in the soul of the Believer

---

[1] Hastings' *Dictionary of the Bible*, article 'Prophecy.'
"The fountain of prophecy was communion with God."
[2] We shall use this term as the correlative of "Prophet."

to which the Prophet can appeal. There must,
in other words, be *continuity* between the experience of the Prophet and that of the Believer if
the divine message is to be accepted: "If you
say you have a revelation from God, I must have
a revelation from God too before I can believe
you[1]." To discover the nature of this two-fold
revelation is the chief task of this chapter, but
for the moment we need notice only the essential
identity of the Prophet's and the Believer's
experience.

The continuity is demonstrable from the facts
of ordinary religious life. Every religious man
believes *communion* with God to be attainable in
prayer. *Inspiration*, too, is a fact of ordinary experience. It is this that accounts for the unique
position which the Bible has always held for
Christians. The Bible has never been entirely
an "Outline" of history or science or a mere
collection of proof-texts. Its value for the ordinary Christian has always lain in its character as
a source of inspiration. Inspiration, again, it is
the aim of preaching and of religious ceremonies
to induce.

It is, then, in virtue of the continuity of the

---

[1] Benjamin Whichcote in W. R. Inge, *The Platonic Tradition in English Religious Thought*, p. 50. Cp. H. H. Wendt,
op. cit. p. 37: "The possession of it (*i.e.* the power of
'intuitive' religious perception) in potency belongs to the
likeness of God which constitutes the innate superiority of
man to the other creatures."

Prophetic experience with his own that the Believer is able to apprehend the Prophetic message: for the Believer, too, is familiar with the two "moments," the sense of communion and the sense of inspiration. The difference must lie in the fact that the Prophet's is a heightened and intensified experience.

"By Inspiration," writes T. H. Sprott, "I understand the quickening and heightening of man's apprehensive powers by the Spirit of God, whereby he is enabled to apprehend the Divine revelation and to become an interpreter of it to his fellows[1]."

Otto regards Prophets (or "diviners," as he calls them) as "especially endowed":

This 'endowment' is the universal disposition on a higher level and at a higher power, differing from it in quality as well as in degree[2].

In the Prophet the sense of communion is deepened, and his inspiration is so intensified as to become *creative*—capable of producing inspiration in others[3].

What is the nature of this creative inspiration?

The oldest view of its nature is indicated by the etymology of the word itself. The "spirit" or "breath" of Yahweh was said to come upon

[1] *Inspiration and the Old Testament*, p. 55.

[2] *Op. cit.* p. 181.

[3] "The test of Inspiration is the power to inspire." Quoted by B. H. Streeter, *Reality*, p. 112.

the Hebrew Prophets. They seemed to be "possessed" by a spirit not their own, which led them to hear, see and do things beyond their natural powers. Even madmen were thought to be inspired. Under inspiration the Prophet would hear the voice of Yahweh ("thus saith the Lord") or behold the assembled powers of heaven.

The singular character of these and like phenomena is now recognised to be explicable in principle without resort to the hypothesis of direct divine interposition. Psychology explains them as due to

the remarkable tendency of primitive thought to express itself in images rather than in concepts, in forms which appeal to the senses and emotions rather than to the intellect, by means of symbolic rather than rational representation[1].

These are simply the forms in which the message is clothed[2]; they cannot be used as "evidences" for its truth.

There is, however, another alleged mode of direct communication with the divine, often styled mysticism[3]. The treatment of this subject

[1] J. S. Huxley, *op. cit.* p. 274.

[2] "They mark no rank of sainthood and indicate no miracle-working power." *Encyclopedia of Religion and Ethics*, article 'Mysticism.'

[3] *E.g.* by W. James (*The Varieties of Religious Experience*) in accordance with his belief that the pathological represents religious experience at the highest power.

The whole question of mysticism is difficult and involved,

is difficult because different writers use the word *mysticism* to connote very different types of experience. William James isolates four characteristics or "marks" of this state of consciousness[1]. Its first mark is Ineffability.

The subject of it immediately says that it defies expression, that no adequate report of its contents can be given in words. It follows from this that it cannot be imparted or transferred to others. In this peculiarity mystical states are more like states of feeling than like states of intellect.

Its second rule is that in spite of its ineffability it is manifested in states which have a "Noetic quality."

Mystical states seem to those who experience them to be also states of knowledge. They are states of insight into depths of truth unplumbed by the discursive intellect.

These two marks are sufficient, says James, to entitle any state of mind to be called mystical, but two further marks are usually found— Transiency, and, finally, Passivity.

Although the oncoming of mystical states may be facilitated by preliminary voluntary operations...yet when the characteristic sort of consciousness once has set

yet it is obvious that the mysticism treated by James differs altogether from both the "subjective" and "objective" types distinguished by Inge in his *Christian Mysticism*. To Inge the "mysticism" of James appears as an irrelevant psychological by-product. See note at end of chapter.

[1] W. James, *op. cit.* pp. 380 f.

in, the mystic feels as if his own will were in abeyance, and indeed sometimes as if he were grasped and held by a superior power.

"Mysticism" bears no necessary relation to moral or intellectual capacity. Something very like it can be artificially stimulated by such methods as are used by psychologists to induce hypnosis. This being so, it is *prima facie* improbable that "mysticism" is a special way of direct communication of knowledge by the divine. This conclusion is confirmed by consideration of the results of "mysticism." The mystical state being essentially incommunicable, when intellectual formulation of results is attempted the results are necessarily contradictory. In the East, for example, mystical knowledge seems to point to an impersonal, in the West to a personal Deity. This fact shows that it is previous theological conceptions that determine the result. Again "mysticism" is an affair of personal satisfaction—it cannot share its experiences with others. We may say, then, that mysticism cannot be regarded as a channel of direct creative inspiration[1].

There is, then, no mode of *direct* access to new religious knowledge. Nor need we seek

[1] This is not to deny that certain mystical states may be states of communion with God. James regards them as states of "contact with a large consciousness," and Prayer has been regarded as the beginning of such a state. All we contend here is that "mysticism" cannot convey *revelatory* knowledge of God.

such access. To regard God as the *cause* of a psychological state is to bring Him into the sphere of phenomena—to use Him to fill up a gap in science.

Science has no need, and indeed, can make no use, in any particular instance, of the theistic hypothesis. That hypothesis is specially applicable to nothing just because it claims to be equally applicable to everything[1].

If religious knowledge is not conveyed in this "direct" way, its source must be sought elsewhere. It must be either a feeling caused by, or a judgment passed upon phenomena. But it cannot lie in a feeling, for a feeling (like a mystical state) can have validity only for the experient: *de gustibus non disputandum*. Can the source then be an intellectual judgment? To suppose this, was the fallacy of that "classical" view which regarded miracles as evidences.

A man encounters an occurrence that is not "natural." ...Since it has actually occurred it must have had a cause, and since it has no "natural" cause, it must (so it is said) have a supernatural one[2].

We saw how this theory broke down—the miracle is a sign only to the eye of faith, it cannot bring conviction to the logical reason. Again, to make intellectual judgments upon

[1] James Ward, *Naturalism and Agnosticism*, 2nd edition, I, p. 23.
[2] R. Otto, *op. cit.* pp. 148 f.

phenomena is the sphere of science and philosophy[1]. The type of judgment we are seeking to identify will of course be made only by a religious man. But it will not therefore be erroneous: it will still remain a valid judgment. A judgment however it must be, for this alone can claim objective validity.

The religious judgment is made when a religious man so interprets phenomena as to discover God. It is of a peculiar character for the reason that in religion the subjective cannot be eliminated. It is this that distinguishes religion from science : in the latter we endeavour to exclude all subjectivity, in the former we can never pass out of it[2]. It follows that the religious judgment is passed rather upon *experience* than phenomena alone.

The religious judgment will be a perception of the reality behind appearances. Where a man is qualified to find this reality, "the universe becomes the revelation of God to him[3]." This will be the privilege of the few. For the rest there will be no Revelation; for

[1] A. Sabatier, *Outlines*, p. 310 : "To know the world as an astronomer or a physicist is not to know it religiously." Cp. *Encyclopedia of Religion and Ethics*, article 'Ritschlianism': "The knowledge of God finds expression in another kind of judgment than that of the theoretical knowledge of the world."

[2] A. Sabatier, *op. cit.* p. 303. Cp. also p. 310: "To know God religiously is to know Him in His relation to us."

[3] S. A. MacDowall, *Evolution, Knowledge and Revelation*, p. 96.

a divine operation only becomes a real Revelation in so far as men in it or by it come to some knowledge of God[1].

There are present to the mind two types of experience: experience of the subjective world of one's own consciousness, and experience of the objective world outside it. God has been apprehended in both these worlds. Some religious geniuses have contemplated the one, some the other.

I. That God should be sought in the *subjective* world was maintained by the Cambridge Platonist John Smith: the place of Revelation is the soul, not nature: "Intra te quaere Deum[2]." At a later date Jacobi declares, "We believe in God, not by reason of nature, which conceals him, but by reason of the supernatural in man[3]." This unfavourable estimate of nature has been reasserted in modern times, when science has seemed to present the world as "indifferent" to all the aspirations of men.

(i) God has been thought by many to reveal himself particularly in the moral life. Thus John Smith says:

Divine truth is better understood, as it unfolds itself in the purity of men's hearts and lives, than in all those subtile niceties into which curious wits may lay it forth[4].

[1] H. H. Wendt, *op. cit.* p. 16.

[2] Caldecott and Mackintosh, *Selections from the Literature of Theism*, p 117.

[3] Quoted by C. C. J. Webb, *Problems in the Relations of God and Man*, p. 56.

[4] Caldecott and Mackintosh, *op. cit.* pp. 122 f.

This view receives great support from the character of the teaching of Jesus. James Martineau regarded this teaching as based upon "moral intuitions," the "self-attesting revelations of the divine mind." For him Revelation is a "descent of the divine into the human in the form of moral intuitions [1]." The whole Liberal Protestant school regards the Christian Revelation in this way.

(ii) In the theory of the religious judgment as a "value-judgment," religious feeling itself is taken as the sphere of consideration. This theory is founded on the essential subjectivity, which we have already noticed, of the religious judgment [2]. Thus Auguste Sabatier says : "We never become conscious of our piety without...perceiving, more or less obscurely, in that very emotion the object and the cause of religion, *i.e.* God [3]." The case is analogous to that of moral judgment; the subject feels obliged, and this obligation itself constitutes the revelation of the moral object that obliges.

To know (the world) religiously is, while taking it

[1] *The Seat of Authority in Religion*, chapter II. Cp. also Wordsworth in one place: "Moral action is that great and only experiment in which all riddles of the most manifold appearances explain themselves." W. R. Inge, *Platonic Tradition*, p. 71.

[2] A. Sabatier, *Outlines*, gives a much clearer account than Ritschl himself of the thesis which we take Ritschl to be maintaining in his theory of the value-judgment.

[3] *Ibid*. p. 308.

as it is, and in no wise contradicting the scientific laws according to which it is governed, to determine its value in relation to the life of the spirit; it is to estimate it according as it is a means, a hindrance or a menace to the progress of that life. In the same way, to know ourselves religiously...is to realise ourselves in our relation both to God and to the world, forcing ourselves to surmount the contradictions from which we suffer, in order that we may attain to unity and peace of mind[1].

(iii) The third way of apprehending God in the inner life is denoted by the term "mysticism" used in a different sense from that we have already examined. In this type of mysticism the aim is practical[2]. The end is not knowledge of God but union with Him. The mystic attempts to find God in the depths of his own inner life. This is possible because

there is...something in the human soul which is unsundered from the Absolute, something which essentially *is* that Reality....The soul can know *super-empirical* reality only because, when it sinks to its deepest centre, it is one with that reality; it is identical with what it knows[3].

The path to this union is called "the mystic way," and the stages in it have been carefully marked out by those who have trodden it. But

[1] *Ibid.* p. 310.
[2] Cp. the definition of Corderius (W. R. Inge, *Christian Mysticism*, p. 335): "Theologia mystica est sapientia experimentalis."
[3] *Encyclopedia of Religion and Ethics*, article 'Mysticism.' In this article this type of mysticism is distinguished as "mysticism," the former type as "mystical experience."

this type of mysticism, like that we have already examined, is *personal* and *non-creative*. The mystics of Christian history [1] have never been Prophets. It is for this reason that mysticism was tolerated, though with a bad grace, by the Church in the Middle Ages: it was not a new source of authority.

II. We now come to the apprehension of God in the objective world.

Religion is convinced not only that the holy and sacred reality is attested by the inward voice of conscience and the religious consciousness, the "still, small voice" of the Spirit in the heart, by feeling, presentiment, and longing, but also that it may be directly encountered in particular occurrences and events, self-revealed in persons and displayed in actions, in a word, that beside the inner revelation from the Spirit, there is an outward revelation of the divine nature [2].

(i) The outward Revelation of God is sought first in *History*. This was the sphere in which the Hebrew Prophets discerned the activity of Yahweh. To persons who are *not* divinatory, History appears to be as "indifferent" as Nature, but for the Prophets "History was a moral

---

[1] Christian mysticism is essentially a mode of "interpretation" and so is examined at this point in our argument. It has always, however, been associated with "mystical experiences," which have come at rare moments as "consolations" and rewards—an ἐπιγιγνόμενόν τι τέλος, as Aristotle would say.

[2] R. Otto, *op. cit.* p. 147.

current[1]," and they drew from it religious lessons.

Only a person can interpret an historical event so as to make it the origin of a new religious movement; only a powerfully spiritual person can give such a movement an ethical impress[2].

(ii) By others, the Revelation of God is found in Nature. These are called by Dr Inge "mystics of the objective type." It is a type characteristic of the period since the Reformation:

An important school of mystics...have turned to the religious study of nature, and have found there the same illumination which the mediaeval ascetics drew from the deep wells of their inner consciousness[3].

For the mystic "all Nature is sacramental and symbolic, linked together by the Mind that created it[4]." This view is especially familiar to readers of Wordsworth. It is well expressed by Charles Kingsley:

The great Mysticism is the belief which is becoming every day stronger with me, that all symmetrical natural objects are types of some spiritual truth or existence. When I walk the fields, I am oppressed now and then with an innate feeling that everything I see has a meaning, if I could but understand it. And this feeling of being surrounded with truths which I cannot grasp

---

[1] Hastings' *Dictionary of the Bible*, article 'Prophecy.'
[2] Baentsch, *Altorientalischer u. Israelitischer Monotheismus* (quoted by W. L. Wardle, *Israel and Babylon*, p. 116).
[3] W. R. Inge, *Christian Mysticism*, p. 245.
[4] *Idem, Platonic Tradition*, p. 73.

amounts to indescribable awe sometimes. Everything seems to be full of God's reflex, if we could but see it[1].

Such a position as this is, as it were, an experimental verification of the Platonic philosophy and also of the philosophy of Berkeley, with its theory of "sign-symbolism."

The Revelation of the divine has been found in all these spheres—subjectively, in the moral life, the religious life, the inner life in general; objectively, in History and Nature. But there is no occasion to limit it to any one of these. "All Nature (and there are few more pernicious errors than that which separates man from Nature) is the language in which God expresses His thoughts[2]." That apprehension of the divine will be most true which finds God in every sphere: "Only by the consideration of the totality of His operations can we acquire a perfect conception of His will and work in relation to us[3]."

The religious judgment, then, can be equated with the mystical apprehension of the divine in Nature, if we use both *mystical* and *Nature* in the widest sense. It is defined in other terms in the generalised theory based upon anthropo-

[1] Quoted by W. R. Inge, *Christian Mysticism*, pp. 341 f.
Kingsley's "awe" is sometimes associated with a mystical experience like that enjoyed by the "subjective" mystic (*v. supra*, p. 83).
[2] W. R. Inge, *Christian Mysticism*, p. 250.
[3] H. H. Wendt, *op. cit.* p. 15.

logical data, which has recently been worked out by Rudolf Otto in *The Idea of the Holy*.

According to Otto, the religious judgment is made by the faculty of "divination." This conception was first made use of by Schleiermacher in his *Discourses on Religion* (1799). It is true that the objective character of divination is obscured in Schleiermacher by his speaking of it as an *intuition, feeling*[1], or *emotion*, and by his making inward sensibility (*Sinn*) the "specific organ of religion[2]." But this terminology is inspired by an excessive dread of rationalism: the term "feeling" seemed to stand for all those elements which "Reason" in the sense of "reasoning" had *frozen out* of religion in the eighteenth century. This leads Schleiermacher to confound the character of the judgment with the "feeling tone" which accompanies it. What Schleiermacher is seeking is really

the faculty or capacity of deeply absorbed *contemplation*, when confronted by the vast, living totality and reality of things as it is in nature and history. Wherever a mind is exposed in a spirit of absorbed submission to impressions

[1] Caldecott and Mackintosh, *op. cit.* p. 265 n.
[2] Some writers accept the term "feeling" as accurate, but attempt to safeguard the objectivity of the feeling: doctrines are generalisations of feeling but not therefore subjective, for the feelings are the result of the operation of the universe, of personal experience, not merely of personal excitability. For the essentially subjective character of feeling, cp. H. Rashdall, *Theory of Good and Evil*, I, chap. vi.

of "the universe," it becomes capable—so he lays it down—of experiencing "intuitions" and "feelings" (*Anschauungen* and *Gefühle*) of something that is, as it were, a sheer overplus, in addition to empirical reality[1].

These intuitions form

the glimpse of an Eternal, in and beyond the temporal and penetrating it, the apprehension of a ground and meaning of things in and beyond the empirical and transcending it. They are *surmises* of a Reality fraught with mystery and momentousness[2].

The "faculty" by which this Reality is perceived[3] is not a sixth sense, but rather a *capacity* —the capacity of making a certain kind of judgment. This is an "aesthetic" rather than a logical judgment, for it is not "worked out in accordance with a clear intellectual scheme[4]," yet it claims objective validity. It is a capacity present *potentially* in all, yet *actually* only in "gifted individuals." These Schleiermacher calls "mediators." "They interpret to man the misunderstood voice of God and reconcile him to the earth and his place therein[5]." In the technical language of Otto they awaken in others "the loftier *a priori* cognitions."

The loftier *a priori* cognitions are such as—while everyone is indeed capable of having them—do not, as experience teaches us, occur spontaneously, but rather

---

[1] R. Otto, *op. cit.* p. 150.　　　[2] *Ibid.* p. 151.

[3] Fries calls it a "faculty of divining the objective teleology of the world," R. Otto, *ibid*.

[4] *Ibid.* p. 152.

[5] Schleiermacher's *Discourses*, ed. J. W. Oman, p. 6.

are "awakened" through the instrumentality of other more highly endowed natures. In relation to these, the universal "predisposition" is merely a faculty of *receptivity* and a *principle of acknowledgement*, not a capacity to produce the cognitions in question for oneself independently. This latter capacity is confined to those specially "endowed." And this "endowment" is the universal disposition on a higher level and at a higher power, differing from it in quality as well as in degree[1].

The terms "specially endowed man," "special divinatory nature," "Mediator" are simply alternative expressions for *Prophet*. We saw at the beginning of the chapter that the experience of the Prophet must be in a sense identical with that of the Believer. The character of this identity is explained by Otto's theory. The Prophet is able to inspire others because they are *potentially* capable of receiving the same inspiration as that which he, with his heightened faculties, has received. *Actually* they can only receive the message which he imparts. Their inspiration is inspiration at *second-hand*.

Summing up our enquiry into the modern view of Revelation, we may say, then, (i) that it proceeds from the human side, regarding religious knowledge, like other knowledge, as the appropriation or discovery of something revealed by God; (ii) that it finds religious discovery to be made by specially endowed men; and (iii) that it regards religious discovery as the apprehension of the divine Reality behind appearances.

[1] R. Otto, *op. cit.* p. 181.

Note on Mystical Experience.

The Prophet's apprehension of the Divine seems often to lead to that "mystical experience" or ecstasy which we have found to be obtainable, on the one hand by the "subjective" (p. 83) and the "objective" (p. 86) mystic, and on the other hand through the agency of drugs or hypnosis (p. 78). This clearly shews that it is a psychological state accompanying any *real* or *supposed* insight into the divine nature. C. E. Raven (*The Creator Spirit*, p. 244 f.) contrasts false and true ecstasy. The former "can be obtained by what Murisier calls simplification, by the annulling of the restraints imposed by the higher centres of the brain . . . . This is the effect of alcohol, and is what, to some extent, happens in hypnosis." The latter is the true ecstasy: "It is unification by synthesis, the attainment of a new relationship by a fully integrated personality. 'All the hundred voices of human desire are here brought to unison.' The field of consciousness is not narrowed, but enlarged; the senses are not inhibited, but sublimated; the intuitions are clarified and harmonised; the will is quickened and fortified."

CHAPTER VIII

The Excellence of Revealed Religion

HAVING thus briefly sketched the modern conception of Revelation, we are now in a position to indicate the character of the apologetic which is to convince the modern mind of "the truth and excellence of Revealed Religion."

We found that the distinction between "natural" and "revealed" religion has no real validity; without the grace of God there could be no knowledge of Him. Yet we were able to give some content to the distinction by using it to express a certain *characteristic* of religion *in general*. We saw that all but the most rudimentary religion was built upon insight into the divine nature attained by specially endowed men or "Prophets"; and we styled religion "revealed" in respect of its character as the product of Prophecy.

The Prophet possesses in a developed form that capacity of apprehending the divine which is present potentially in all men. It follows that by vindicating the reality of this apprehension we shall be vindicating the revealed character of religion. It is on account of the existence of this capacity that we can speak of "Revealed Religion." Religion—in the widest sense, all religion—is "revealed" in virtue of having for its basis this apprehension of the divine.

It is in fact upon this point that the modern attack on religion is concentrated. Former generations of anti-Christian writers assailed external and internal evidences: to-day it is "the objectivity of religious experience" that is impugned.

The psychological attack on religion asserts that religious experience is adequately accounted for without recourse to an explanation outside psychology. It proceeds by assimilating religious experience to experience in hallucinations and dreams. In accounting for the phenomena of dreaming it is demonstrably false to assert that the mind is perceiving objective reality, and accordingly the explanation is sought in the subjective sphere. But this interpretation of dream phenomena lies outside the sphere of psychology. Psychology can never give a verdict on questions of ontology. The point wherein dreams differ from religious experiences is in the witness of other observers. Since we consider "objective" only that which is perceived in common by several observers, what is seen by one person but not by others is denied objectivity. The evidence against the reality of dream-phenomena is thus brought from *outside* the dream experience. It follows in the case of religious experience that psychology, which is competent to examine the experience itself, is incompetent to deny, or indeed to assert the reality of the Object felt to be experienced. Denial can come from Philosophy alone[1].

The sceptical attitude towards the object of religious experience is due partly to the unique character of its Object. God is "not an object of possible experience." It is therefore not possible to verify the existence of God by the evidence of the senses; and in the absence of such evidence, the assertions of the religious consciousness are inevitably regarded as more "subjective" than those of another mode of consciousness.

This is one cause of the distrust of religious experience. Another cause is revealed by epistemology. For convenience of thought, the unity of experience can be severed into a dichotomy of subject and object[2]. In this severance, Religion fares worse than other modes of experiences: if we compare Religion with the other three great activities[3] of man's higher nature, we can see at once how its Object seems to suffer in point of verifiability. In the case of *Aesthetics*, the human faculty involved is the *aesthetic sense* and the object is *beauty*; in *Ethics*, the faculty is the *moral consciousness* and the object the *moral law*; in the *Logical* sphere the faculty is the *intellect* and the object

[1] This brings us to the important principle of Joseph Butler: the principle that revealed theology presupposes natural theology. If there is no God, there can be no apprehension of God.

[2] Cp. James Ward, *Naturalism and Agnosticism*, II, *passim*.

[3] F. v. Hügel, *Essays and Addresses*, I, p. 53.

logical order. In Religion the faculty involved is the religious sense, or the faculty of "divination," and the Object God. Now there is seldom any question as to the objectivity of Beauty or Logical Order. The objectivity of the Moral Law has indeed been constantly called in question, but it is very difficult in practice to treat it as non-existent. The religious sense, on the other hand, seems to posit an Object which "a little philosophy" is entitled to reject altogether.

The reason for this facile rejection is clear. It is not until recent times that the connection between the religious sense and its object has received any scientific examination whatsoever. Before Schleiermacher, the existence of the Object of religion was always first "demonstrated" philosophically, and only afterwards brought into connection with that sense which naïvely posits it. Thus the connection always appeared an artificial one. The philosophy of religion, in effect, rejected the witness of the religious sense and substituted a conception of its own. It is not until quite recently that there has been a vindication of the objectivity of religious experience upon the basis of that experience itself. The existence of the aesthetic sense has always been considered a powerful argument for the objectivity of Beauty; the moral sense has been regarded as the chief indication of a Moral Law; but the intimations of the naïve religious consciousness were put away as soon as the simple believer became an apologist, and the Object of the religious sense has always been proved by metaphysics.

But the religious consciousness is surely entitled to the same treatment as the other "highest activities." Each of these posits, and is generally allowed by philosophy to retain, something "given¹." There is no valid reason why what is "given" to the religious sense should alone be denied reality.

Only if we show how and why the logical, the aesthetic and the ethical life can alone be trusted and not the religious life also, where it supplies what those three lives all severally seek, can we consistently accept the deep-lying testimony of the logical, aesthetic, and ethical lives, and, nevertheless, refuse or explain away the central witness of the religious life².

The above argument has been devoted to establishing the "truth" of Revealed Religion. There are two main considerations which establish its "excellence."

We have seen that until the development of a critique of religious experience the metaphysical argument for the existence of God was necessarily the only³ one. But this metaphysical argument has always been felt to be unsatisfactory. There has constantly been difficulty in

¹ The term is v. Hügel's, *op. cit.* p. 56.
² *Ibid.* p. 55.
³ The existence of God could not legitimately be proved from "Revelation," since this would be argument in a circle. In spite of this there have always been attempts to use such an argument.

identifying the God of Philosophy with the God of Revelation. The Absolute is not the Personal God that we worship, the Almighty Artificer is not the loving Father. But if religion be founded upon experience, this discrepancy is not present. We proceed in this case not from something less than God to God, but from God to God[1]. By following the guidance of religious experience we choose the better part.

The content of religious experience thus is "excellent," but the form in which it is made available is excellent too. Both scientific and religious knowledge are advanced by great minds. In the case of the former, however, the mind is all that matters. Ideally, the scientist needs only a mind; his other faculties are but hindrances to his work. But no one can be a Prophet by simply "having the mind." The Prophet must use all his faculties—his heart, soul and mind—in finding out "the living God[2]." Science is the

[1] Prof. A. E. Taylor, "The Vindication of Religion" in *Essays Catholic and Critical*. Taylor recognises three possible methods of approach to the Object of Religion—from Nature to God, from Man to God, and from God to God. The last named is the way of religious experience.

[2] It is the qualifications of the Prophet that in the modern apologetic represent the old "criteria" of Revelation. They may be summed up as follows:

(i) Moral Goodness: Cp. "Blessed are the pure in heart, for they shall see God."

"The Scripture is wont to set forward a good life as the prolepsis and fundamental principle of Divine science." (John Smith, in Caldecott and Mackintosh, *Selections*, p. 115.)

work of persons, religion the work of personalities. It is because the Prophet is a special
personality that he is the most "excellent"
instrument of Revelation. There is a revelation
of God in all His creation for those who can
read it. The philosopher, the scientist, the artist
—all these can construct a "Natural Religion"
for themselves ; but Revealed Religion is open
only to those who accept the Prophet as the
revealer of God.

What shall we say of that religion which alone
was once wont to be called "Revealed"? Christianity is the revealed religion *par excellence*. In
its Prophet the nature of God seems to be so
fully revealed that He has for us the religious
value of God[1].

"We can look, beyond the Prophet, to one
in whom is found the Spirit in all its plenitude,
and who at the same time in his person and in
his performance is become most completely the
object of divination, in whom Holiness is recognised apparent.

"Such a one is more than Prophet. He is
the Son[2]."

(ii) Sanity: Cp. Plato's *Phaedrus*, 248 D (quoted in C. C. J.
Webb, *Problems*) where ecstasy is placed lowest of all forms
of divination.

(iii) Ability to communicate Inspiration: "The test of
inspiration is the power to inspire" (quoted in Streeter,
Reality, p. 112).

[1] W. B. Selbie, *Schleiermacher*, p. 259.

[2] Otto, *op. cit.* p. 182.

BIBLIOGRAPHY

PREFACE

The Cambridge Historical Register.
PARKINSON, RICHARD. *The Hulsean Lectures for* 1838.
The Dictionary of National Biography. Article JOHN HULSE.

PART ONE

Chapters I and II

HASTINGS' *Encyclopedia of Religion and Ethics.* Article
'Prophecy.'
FARRAR, F. W. *A History of Interpretation.*
HATCH, E. *The Influence of Greek Ideas and Usages upon the
Christian Church.*
HASTINGS' *Dictionary of the Bible.* Article 'Prophecy.'
KIDD, B. J. *A History of the Church to* 461 A.D., vol. I.
TIXERONT, J. *Histoire des Dogmes,* 10ième édition.
Encyclopaedia Biblica. Article 'Prophecy.'

Chapter III

ALEXANDER, B. D. *A Short History of Philosophy.*
AQUINAS, ST THOMAS. *Summa Theologiae. Summa contra
Gentiles.*
HARRIS, C. R. S. *Duns Scotus,* vol. I.
GILSON, E. *La Philosophie au Moyen Age.*
PRINGLE-PATTISON, A. S. *Encyclopaedia Britannica.* Article
'Scholasticism.'
POOLE, R. L. *Illustrations of the History of Medieval Thought
and Learning.* (2nd ed.)
WEBB, C. C. J. *Studies in the History of Natural Theology.*
WULF, M. DE. *Histoire de la Philosophie Médiévale.*

Chapter IV

BURTT, E. A. *The Metaphysical Foundations of Modern Physical Science.*

BURY, J. B. *A Short History of the Freedom of Thought.*

BUTLER, JOSEPH. *The Analogy of Religion, Natural and Revealed.*

LOCKE, JOHN. *An Essay concerning the Human Understanding.*

PALEY, WILLIAM. *A View of the Evidences of Christianity*[1].

PATTISON, MARK. Article in 'Essays and Reviews[2].'

PFLEIDERER, OTTO. *The Philosophy of Religion,* vol. I.

SPOONER, W. *Joseph Butler.*

STEPHEN, LESLIE. *History of English Thought in the Eighteenth Century,* vol. I.

Sylloge Confessionum[3].

WORDSWORTH, C. *Christian Institutes,* vol. I.

Chapter V

POWELL, BADEN. Article in 'Essays and Reviews.'

WATSON, JOHN. *Selections from Kant.*

PART TWO

Chapters VI—VIII

CALDECOTT, A. *The Philosophy of Religion.*

CALDECOTT, A. and MACKINTOSH, H. R. *Selections from the Literature of Theism.*

EDGHILL, E. A. *The Revelation of the Son of God.*

EUCKEN, R. *The Truth of Religion.*

FIGGIS, J. N. *The Gospel and Human Needs.*

HERRMANN, W. *Systematic Theology.*

HÜGEL, F. VON. *Essays and Addresses,* First Series.

HUXLEY, JULIAN S. *Religion without Revelation.*

---

[1] Ed. E. A. Lytton, S.P.C.K. 1901.   [2] 12th edition.
[3] Oxford, 1827.

INGE, W. R. *Faith and Its Psychology.*
—— *The Platonic Tradition in English Religious Thought.*
—— *Christian Mysticism.*
JAMES, WILLIAM. *The Varieties of Religious Experience.*
McDOWALL, S. A. *Evolution, Knowledge and Revelation.*
MONTAGUE, W. P. *The Ways of Knowing.*
OMAN, J. W. Schleiermacher's *Speeches on Religion.*
OTTO, RUDOLF. *The Idea of the Holy.*
POWICKE, F. J. *The Cambridge Platonists.*
SABATIER, A. *Outlines of a Philosophy of Religion.*
SANDAY, W. *The Oracles of God.*
SEEBERG, R. *Revelation and Inspiration.*
SELBIE, W. B. *Schleiermacher.*
SPROTT, T. H. *Inspiration and the Old Testament.*
STREETER, B. H. *Reality.*
WEBB, C. C. J. *Problems in the Relations of God and Man.*
WENDT, H. H. *The Idea and Reality of Revelation.*

For EU product safety concerns, contact us at Calle de José Abascal, 56–1°,
28003 Madrid, Spain or eugpsr@cambridge.org.

www.ingramcontent.com/pod-product-compliance
Ingram Content Group UK Ltd.
Pitfield, Milton Keynes, MK11 3LW, UK
UKHW020312140625
459647UK00018B/1844

* 9 7 8 1 1 0 7 6 6 2 2 1 6 *